SPLENDOURS OF RAJASTHAN PAINTINGS

GULISTAN OF ALWAR SCHOOL

SPLENDOURS OF RAJASTHAN PAINTINGS

GULISTAN OF ALWAR SCHOOL

Neeru Misra

MANOHAR
2008

First published 2008

ISBN 978-81-7304-788-6

Published by
Ajay Kumar Jain *for*
Manohar Publishers & Distributors,
4753/23, Ansari Road, Daryaganj,
New Delhi 110 002

Design and typesetting at
Karmic Design, New Delhi 110 091

Printed at
Salasar Imaging Systems
Delhi 110 035

To
Lord who has bestowed in Shagun
unfathomable joys on all of us

CONTENTS

FOREWORD

सत्यमेव जयते

Dr. Karan Singh
MEMBER OF PARLIAMENT
(RAJYA SABHA)

3, Nyaya Marg
Chanakyapuri
New Delhi - 110 021

Rajasthan is one of our most colourful States, rich in historical, archaeological and artistic heritage. It has made a noble contribution to the multi-faceted, pluralistic cultural heritage of India. The rulers of Rajasthan were great patrons of art, during and after the Moghul period. Many artists took refuge there and produced some of their best work, and the painters, specially of Bundi, Kota, Mewar, Marwar, Bikaner and Jaipur, acquired great skill.

The Rajasthan's School of Alwar and Tijara and the atelier of Banni Singh produced some outstanding paintings including an illustrated *Gulistan* of Sheikh Sa'adi. This book by Dr. Neeru Misra deals specifically with the nineteenth-century art of the Alwar School and the remarkable *Gulistan* paintings. It is a work of painstaking research which will be welcomed by students of art history as well as by the general reader interested in the rich cultural heritage of India.

Basant Panchami
11 February 2008

KARAN SINGH

PREFACE

SHEIKH SA'ADI was born in AD 1194. He was a close associate of Sheikh Shihab ud Din Suhrawardy and Sheikh Abdul Faraj Abdul Rahman Ibn Jowzi, a disciple of Gilani, a student of the celebrated Nizamiya University of Baghdad, an ardent follower of the path of the Sufis and having affiliations with the *naqshbandis*. He travelled widely from Baghdad to Central Asia, India, Yemen, Ethiopia and Mecca, and also spent a part of his life as the captive of the Franks in Syria. Sa'adi acquired a rich experience in life and visited many important hamlets in North Africa and Anatolia, before finally settling at Shiraz in AD 1256. His literary journey started from the point his physical journey ended, and soon his writings became popular in far off lands. Not only his tomb in Shiraz became a shrine in the days to come, to be visited by many faithful, but the profundity of his *mathnawis*, *qasidas* and *ghazals* also echoed and reverberated for centuries and are revisited by thirsty minds seeking an answer even today.

Rich and poor, learned and ignorant, young and old, male and female, brave and weak — the characters of his lucid and pragmatic anecdotes embedded in his narratives to elaborate the principles of a moral life have been identified by all readers and admirers of Sa'adi throughout the millennium. "In life beauty perishes, but not in art" said Leonardo Da Vinci and in this lies the secret of the mystic eternity of Sa'adi. Translated into several languages, painted innumerable times by the Shiraz, Herat, Bukhara, Mughal and Rajput schools; the manuscript of *Gulistan* originally composed in the thirteenth-century, has been gifted and possessed with passion. It has adorned the personal collections of the royalty as a status symbol and the nineteenth-century principality of Alwar, having nothing in common with the Persian culture as it existed six hundred years ago, faded in the layers of history, found commissioning *Gulistan* as an authentic expression of an imperial signature.

The European interest in *Gulistan* and other works of Sa'adi have been equally instrumental in its revival in the regional kingdoms that emerged after the Mughal Empire had shrunk and disintegrated. The first known translation of *Gulistan* was published from Amsterdam in 1651 by George Gentius, who made the great work known to the Western world. The 1806 translation by Francis Gladwin was widely published, in many countries including UK, US and India. It was followed by a translation by James Dumoulin in 1807 from Calcutta. A more simple and prosaic translation by James Ross was published in 1823. The interest in the works of Sa'adi in the next few decades saw several other translations by scholars including M. Semelet, Edward B. Eastwick, John T. Platts, R.F. Burton, L.W. Costello, Edward Rehatsek and R.P. Anderson.

I have found the translation by Ross most simple and close to the manuscript of the Alwar School. Closest to being literal, this translation also has a valuable essay on the life of Sa'adi that I have appended to this study for the benefit of the readers. While basing the details of the episodes connected with the paintings on Ross's translation, I have included the variations noticed in other translations as well.

The art of Rajasthan is deeper than any ocean. A lifetime is too small to fully enjoy it. From the awe-inspiring rock paintings of Allaniya dating back to more than thirty-five thousand years to the creations of the present-day painters in the ateliers, workshops and amateur pursuits spread in the *dhanis*, villages and cities all over the state, the kaleidoscope has no parallel. Every traditional household has a rich collection, inviting to be seen and relished. This small work is an attempt to appreciate the glimpse of the rich land of rulers. I consider it my great privilege to have been able to see some of the masterpieces of Rajasthani paintings. I express my gratitude to the Department of Archaeology and Museums, Government of Rajasthan and the officers of the Alwar Museum for having made available the transparencies of *Gulistan*, without which this study would have been impossible.

New Delhi NEERU MISRA
May 2008

ACKNOWLEDGEMENTS

Department of Archeology and Museums,
Government of Rajasthan.

Excerpts reprinted by permission from
The Gulistan of Sadi, translated by Edward B.
Eastwick (The Octagon Press Ltd., London).

Emergence of Alwar and its Art

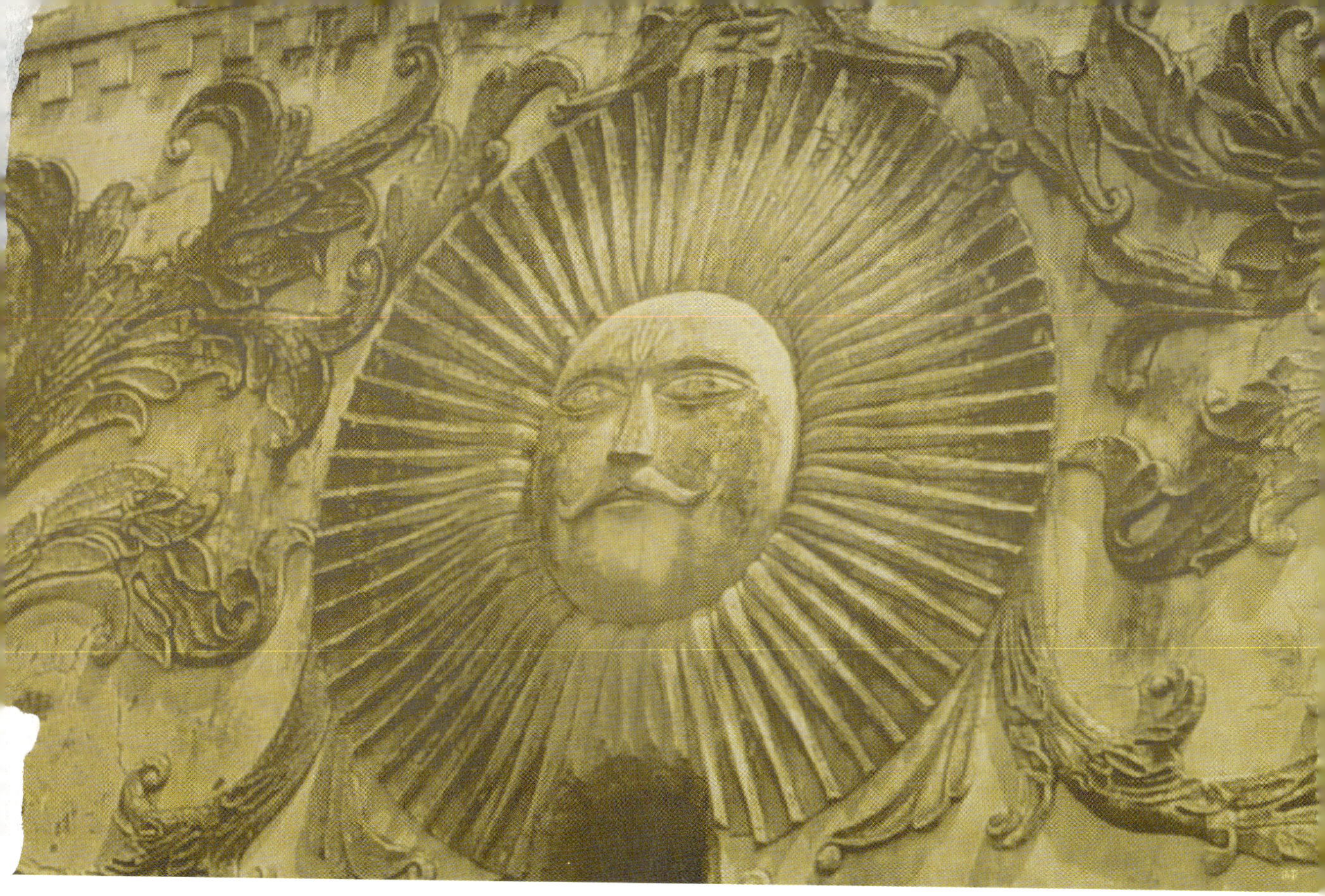

Royal Insignia of the State of Alwar

HISTORY OF ALWAR STATE

ALWAR DISTRICT is situated between 27° 4′ and 28° 4′ north latitude and 76° 7′ and 77° 13′ east longitude in the north-east of Rajasthan. Its length from south to north is about 135 km and breadth from east to west is about 110 km. Gurgaon and Bharatpur districts on the north and north-east and Mahendragarh district on the north-west bind it. On its south-west lies the capital city of Jaipur and on the south the district of Sawai-Madhopur.

The present-day city of Alwar has a historical past. Ancient sources mention a certain kingdom of Uluk, established by the legendary Prince of the Mahabharata by the same name. The name of the region was later distorted and came to be known as Ulur.[1] Some others attribute the name to Alaghurai, son of the ruler of Amber, who founded the principality as Alpur.[2] However, the first mentions of the name Alwar are found in the travelogues of Ferishta, who visited the place during the last decade of the twelfth century.[3]

The study of Rajasthan as a distinct cultural space with identifiable cultural patterns started emerging from the early twentieth century. Tod's Annals and Antiquities of Rajasthan could be referred as one such step in this direction, but it was mainly concerned with regional narration of the political space, loosely referred to as Rajasthan. However, in the initial years of study of sub-regional cultural systems of the Indian subcontinent, language, ethnic patterns, political processes and religion superseded the study of art, literature and music.[4] Even so, the earlier introspections started with the study of the mapping of linguistic commonalities.[5]

The political delineation of Rajasthan was first attempted by the Mughals, when Akbar reorganized the administrative units and created the *subah* of Ajmer in AD 1594 . Though, the rulers of Rajasthan had already aligned with the Mughals and many of them had sustained and regular interactions with the Mughal courts, the subah of Ajmer became one of the gateways for facilitating the formation of an overlapping layer of Mughal culture on the region of Rajasthan.

For administrative convenience, Akbar divided the district of Mewat into two parts, Alwar and Tijara. The fort of Alwar predates the Mughals, and was used as a garrison by Akbar for its strategic importance.[6] Aurangzeb gifted the premises to Sawai Jaisingh, the Rajput ruler of Amber, in recognition of his support for the Prince in the war of succession, but later took it back for strategic considerations on the advice of Iftikhar Khan. When the Mughal hold weakened on the region, the Jat ruler Surajmal of Bharatpur occupied the fort in AD 1756, a position he held for almost two decades.

During the first half of the eighteenth century, the politically decadent Mughal Empire, unleashed several smaller principalities.[7] The Rajput rebellions of Khairabad and Ghazipur were the beginnings of the independence of the Rajputs, who had been used by the Mughals against other groups.[8] The privileged land-holdings formed blocs and consolidated their positions as kingdoms in the years that followed.[9]

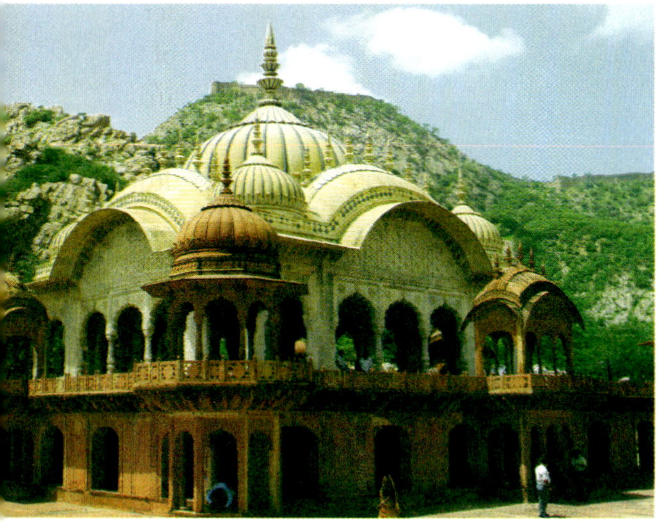

Chhatri of *Moosi Rani*: The patronage and promotion of arts on the lines of the imperial Mughals were used as a means by the rulers of Alwar to enhance their status and legitimacy.

The weakening of the central authority of the Mughals in Rajasthan brought to the fore many mutual internal rivalries and competitions. The regions of eastern Rajasthan saw the resurgence of the "inherent tensions" in the kinship and political fabric of the region.[10] Consequently, the states of Jaipur, Kota, Bundi, Jaisalmer, Bikaner, Dungarpur, Alwar, Tijara and numerous others emerged supported by a third player, the British. These newly emerging kingdoms established their legitimacy by emulating the principles and methodologies of governance employed by the imperial powers, the Mughals and the British. Alwar was in fact the first Rajput state to seek patronage of the "fledgling" British Empire, though at a cost not always fair and palatable.[11]

The founder of the modern kingdom of Alwar was Pratap Singh Naruka, who belonged to the Naruka branch of the Kachhwaha *kul* of Amber rulers, controlling the kingdom of Jaipur. The state of Jaipur was passing through a succession crisis after the untimely demise of Madho Singh in AD 1768.[12] Pratap Singh established the new kingdom of Alwar by declaring it an independent state through carefully initiated steps leading to a gradual severing of the relations from Jaipur, and at the same time without inviting complete estrangement.[13] Machedi was an important *jagir* gifted by Akbar to Kalyan Singh, the predecessor of Pratap Singh, in recognition of his victory over the impregnable fort of Alwar. As a descendent of Kalyan Singh, Pratap Singh inherited the *jagir* of Machedi at the age of 16 years. Traditionally, however, the *jagirdar* of Machedi was subservient to the state of Jaipur. Pratap Singh heightened his influence and authority by inter-playing the rivalry between the Rajput state of

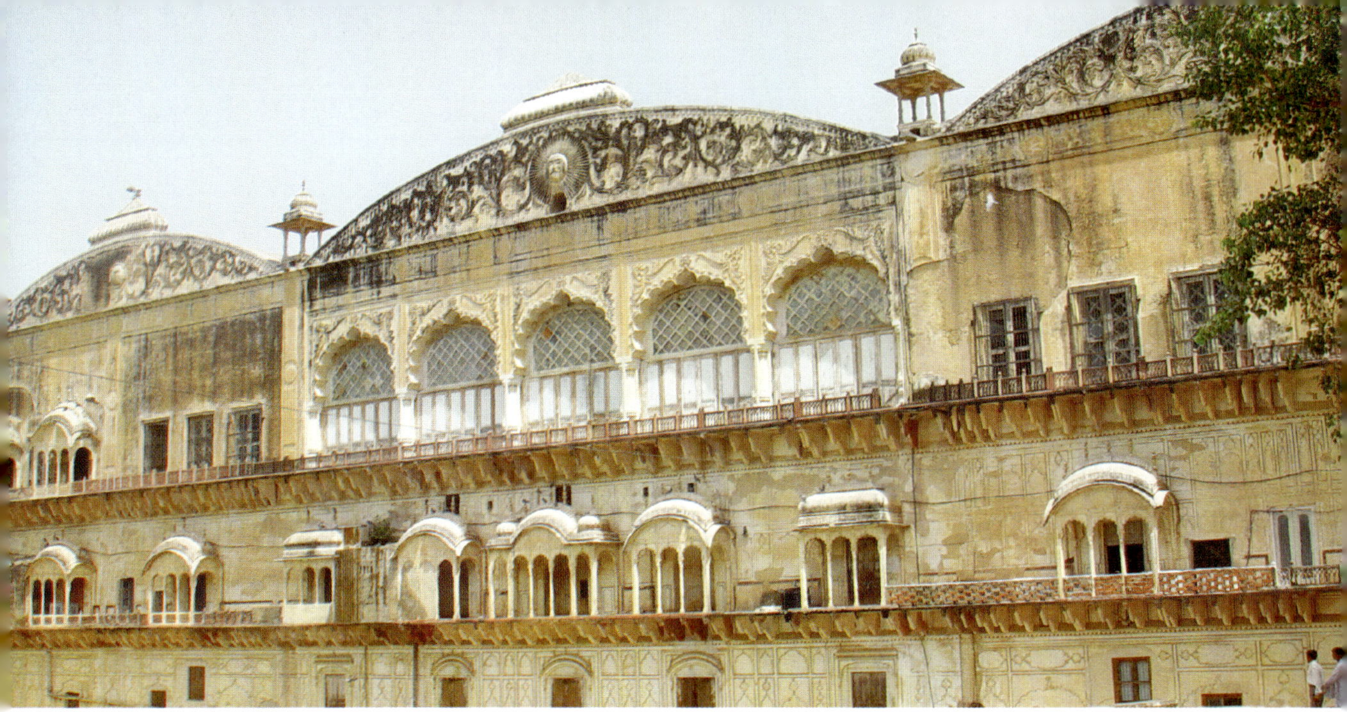

Palace of Bakhtawar Singh, now housing Government Office and Museum

Jaipur and the Jat state of Bharatpur. His support to Mughal noble Najaf Khan in ousting the Jat occupancy of Bharatpur in AD 1775, fetched him the reward of the title of Rao Raja Bahadur, a *mansab* of 5000 and the independent *jagir* of Machedi. Thus, Pratap Singh got the recognition of an independent ruler, free from the fetters of the state of Jaipur. During the same year, the garrison of Alwar fort, under the occupancy of the Jat state of Bharatpur, approached Pratap Singh with a complaint that the Jats had not paid the soldiers their salary for a long time, and if Pratap Singh was agreeable to footing their salary bills, the soldiers would shift their loyalty to him. Pratap Singh readily accepted the proposal, and secured the occupation of the fort of Alwar without war.

Occupation of the fort of Alwar was an important landmark in the establishment of the kingdom by Pratap Singh, who entered the fort on Monday, the 25 December 1775, with great fanfare. He declared Alwar as his capital and fought minor battles to gain control over a number of small satellite towns and villages for the next sixteen years. When he died in AD 1791 at the age of 51 years, his esteem and power were reckoned at par with the kingdoms of Jaipur and Jodhpur.

Pratap Singh had sixteen long years to himself to establish the foundations of the new dynasty at a geo-strategic location in the mountainous territory in the north-east of Jaipur. The nascent kingdom of Alwar was equiproximate from Delhi and Jaipur. At the time of his death, his kingdom comprised the then districts of Thanagazi, Rajgarh, Malakhera, Ajabgarh, Baldeogarh, Kankwari, Alwar, Ramgarh and Lachhmangarh, and areas around Behror and Bansur.

Two interlinked approaches were necessary to establish the legitimacy and acceptance of the new kingdom. First was the crafting of the web of alliances and networks to make the nascent state impervious.[14] The second was to establish its entity at par with the other surrounding imperial states by promoting art, culture and other intangible forms of symbolic projections.[15] Thus, the patronage and promotion of arts on the lines of the imperial Mughals were used as a means by the rulers of Alwar to "enhance their status and legitimacy".[16]

The scenic location of Palace Complex

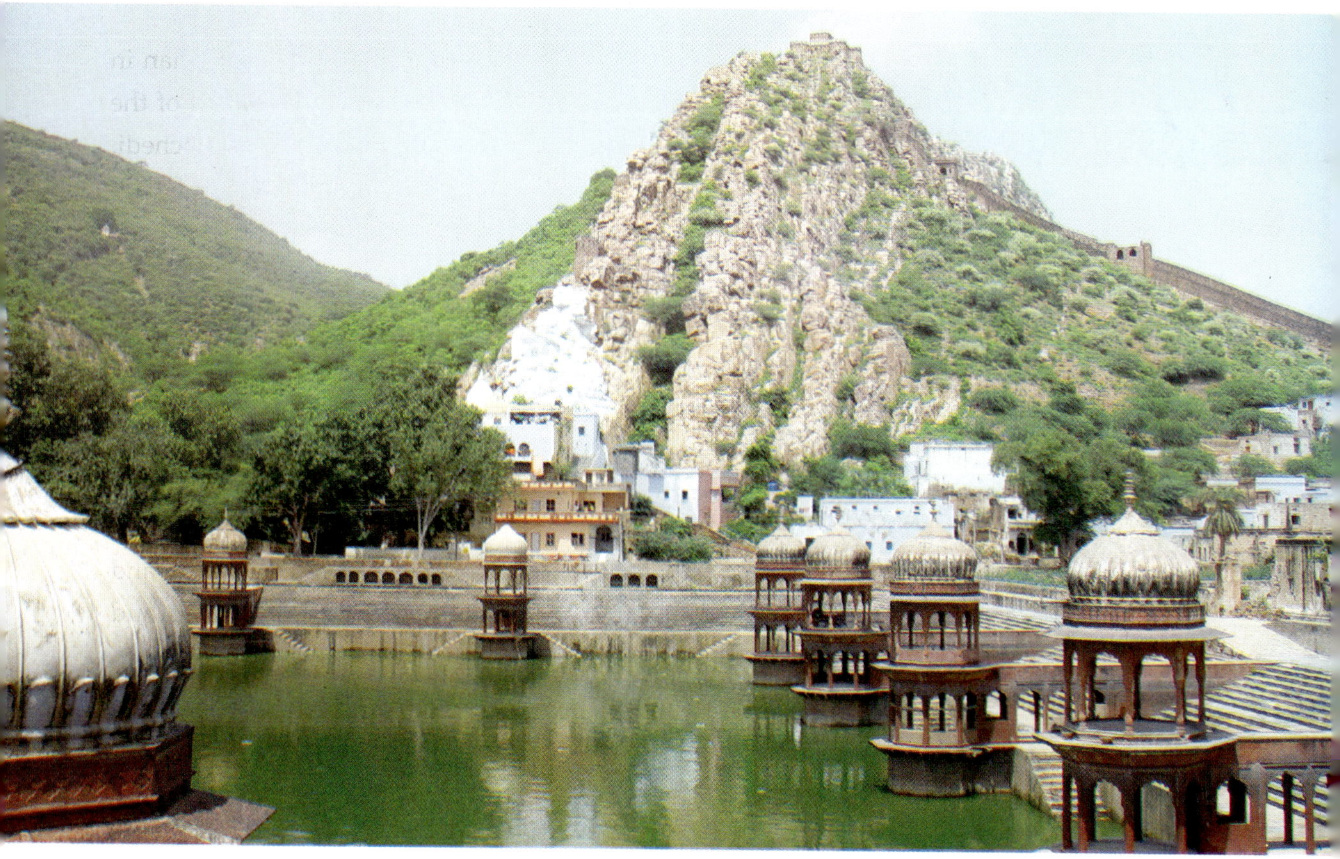

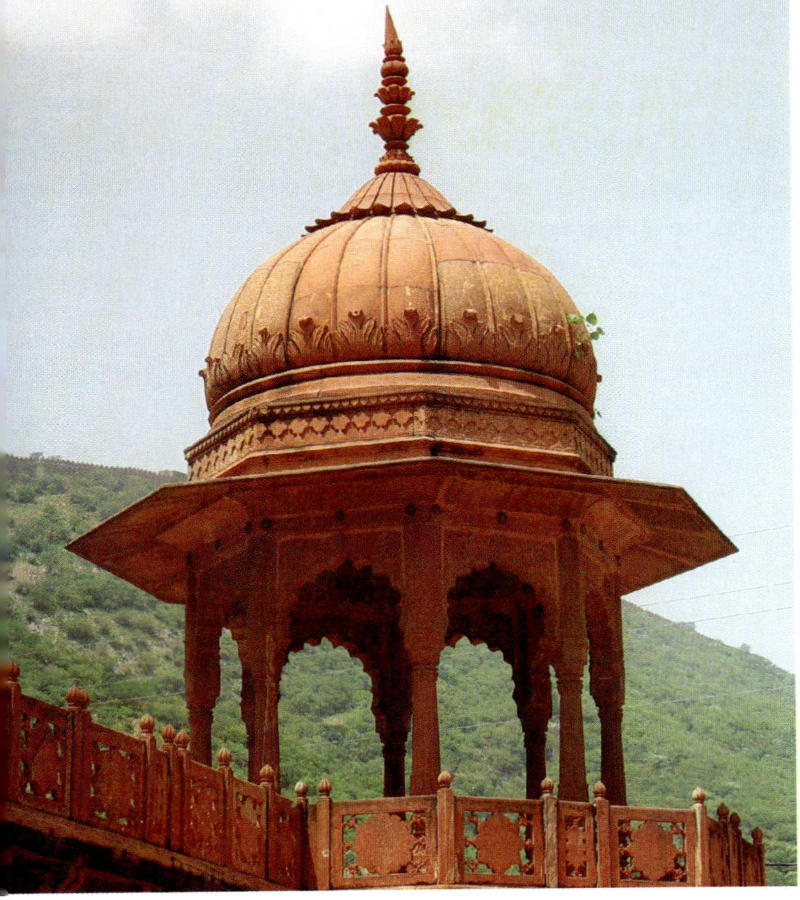

Intricate work on the *chhatri of* Moosi Rani

Pratap Singh was succeeded by his adopted son, Bakhtawar Singh, who was only 15 years old in AD 1791, at the time of the untimely demise of the founder of the kingdom of Alwar. Maharao Raja Bakhtawar Singh was surrounded by foes on all sides. The kingdom of Jaipur considered Alwar a natural tutelage, the ruler of Bharatpur looked for an early opportunity to win back the strategic fort last held by their ruler Surajmal, the Marathas saw the possibility of avenging the reverses suffered during the time of Pratap Singh, and the Mughals at Delhi planned their own share of the spoils out of the newly formed state. Bakhtawar Singh found a promising ally in the British and he extended a crucial support to Lord Lake during the British campaign against the Marathas in the battle of Laswari in Alwar territory, when his troupes assisted Lord in finally breaking the Maratha and Jat alliance. As a consequence, in 1803, the First Treaty of Offensive and Defensive Alliance was signed between the State of Alwar and the East India Company. Thus, Alwar was the first princely State in India to enter into a strategic treaty with the East India Company.

Bakhtawar Singh ruled for almost a quarter of a century, and adopted several measures to establish his royalty. One of the symbols of royalty adopted as a posthumous memorabilia was the performance of sati by Rani Moosi, the widow of Bakhtawar Singh and the subsequent raising of the *chhatri* or the cenotaph of the deceased couple. The scenic location, carvings and architecture of the edifice all combine to impart it a royal signature.

Banni Singh[17] was a minor in AD 1815[18] and ascended the throne jointly with his stepbrother Balwant Singh. Balwant Singh was the son of a Muslim concubine, Paswan Moosi. The Muslim nobility supported the claims of Balwant Singh and drew support from Delhi. The Rajputs supported Banni Singh and the rivalries surfaced in a bitter way in AD 1825 when both came of age. Finally, it was the British intervention, which recognized Banni Singh as the ruler of Alwar and Balwant Singh as the master of the Muslim dominated territory of the partitioned region of Tijara.[19]

That, Banni Singh drew heavily on the administrative expertise of the remnants of the Mughal kingdom of Delhi, still regarded as the ideal is known from contemporary records. The Imperial Gazetteer mentions that Government of Alwar State had "previously been carried on without any system. But with the aid of certain Musalmans introduced from Delhi and appointed ministers in 1838, great changes were made. The land revenue began to be collected in cash instead of kind and civil and criminal courts were established."

ART OF BOOK

ART OF BOOK has come a long way in India. Ancient Indian knowledge was preserved through the oral traditions with a "complex mnemonic system" perfected from about the fifteenth century BC. Gradually, with the influence of the traders, and with the necessity of keeping the accounts, symbols, language and scripts evolved along with medium like tree leaves, metallic leaves, rocks, plates and tablets. Buddhist texts speak about the collection of leaves or *panna* used for recording knowledge from as early as the fifth century BC, and which continued to be used in south India until as late as the nineteenth century AD.[20] Held together with a chord in the form of a book, it has been the base for artists, writers and the elite to record their excellence in calligraphy and illustrated expressions. The standardization of written words and the art of calligraphy in India evolved with the necessity of the Buddhist and Jain preachers to conserve their teachings as accurately as possible for posterity. Paper was in regular use in China from as early as the sixth century AD. However, it took a long time to cross the Himalayas, and could find regular use in India only as late as the thirteenth century AD. One of the main reasons for an early non-proliferation of the art of paper-making in India has been the raw material, which was derived from the plants that grew in the Himalayas.

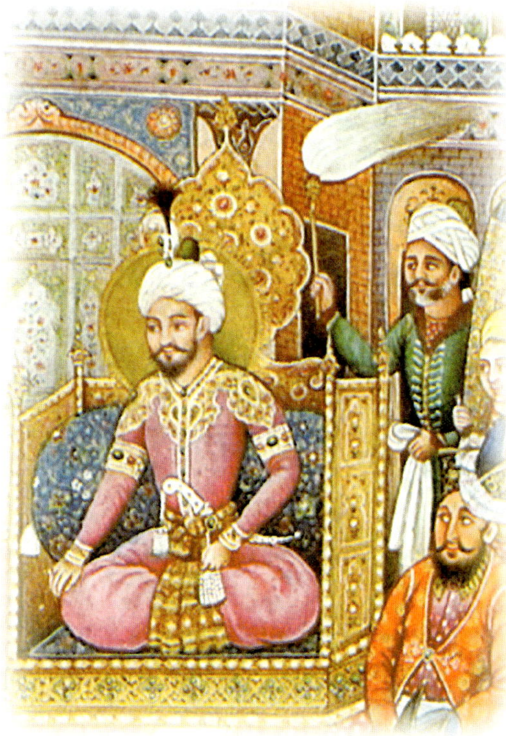

King listening to *Gulistan* — detail of painting 2

While the introduction of paper was a revolution in the art of illustrated manuscript writing, it also changed the aspect ratios. The palm leaves were in the *pothi* format with a ratio of 1 : 3 between the height and the width; this gradually changed and by fifteenth century, the width shrunk to be smaller than the height.[21] The binding of the paper sheets with leather cover started in Kashmir some time around the early fifteenth century. It was only in the sixteenth century in the Mughal ateliers that the regular binding styles emerged with "gold tooling, stamping, gilding, and also pasteboard covers painted and lacquered instead of being covered with leather".[22]

To prevent the decay of the manuscript from termites, white ants and natural decadents like humidity, protective cloth and leather covers were specially crafted. Sometimes special boxes of wood were also made for greater protection.

The establishment of the Sultanate at Delhi opened also the cultural contacts with Persia and Central Asia where the art of book had already developed. It is now evident that Sultans at Delhi and provincial kingdoms maintained their own studios, though in much smaller magnitude and excellence than what was achieved under Akbar. Humayun, who during his days of exile stayed as a guest of the Shah of Iran and encountered the fully mature art of Shiraz and Bukhara, in fact was the founder of the traditions of the Mughal atelier. With the turn of his fortunes and return to the throne of Agra, Humayun brought with him the two great artists of the time, Mir Sayyid Ali and Abdus Samad, who had gladly agreed to join the

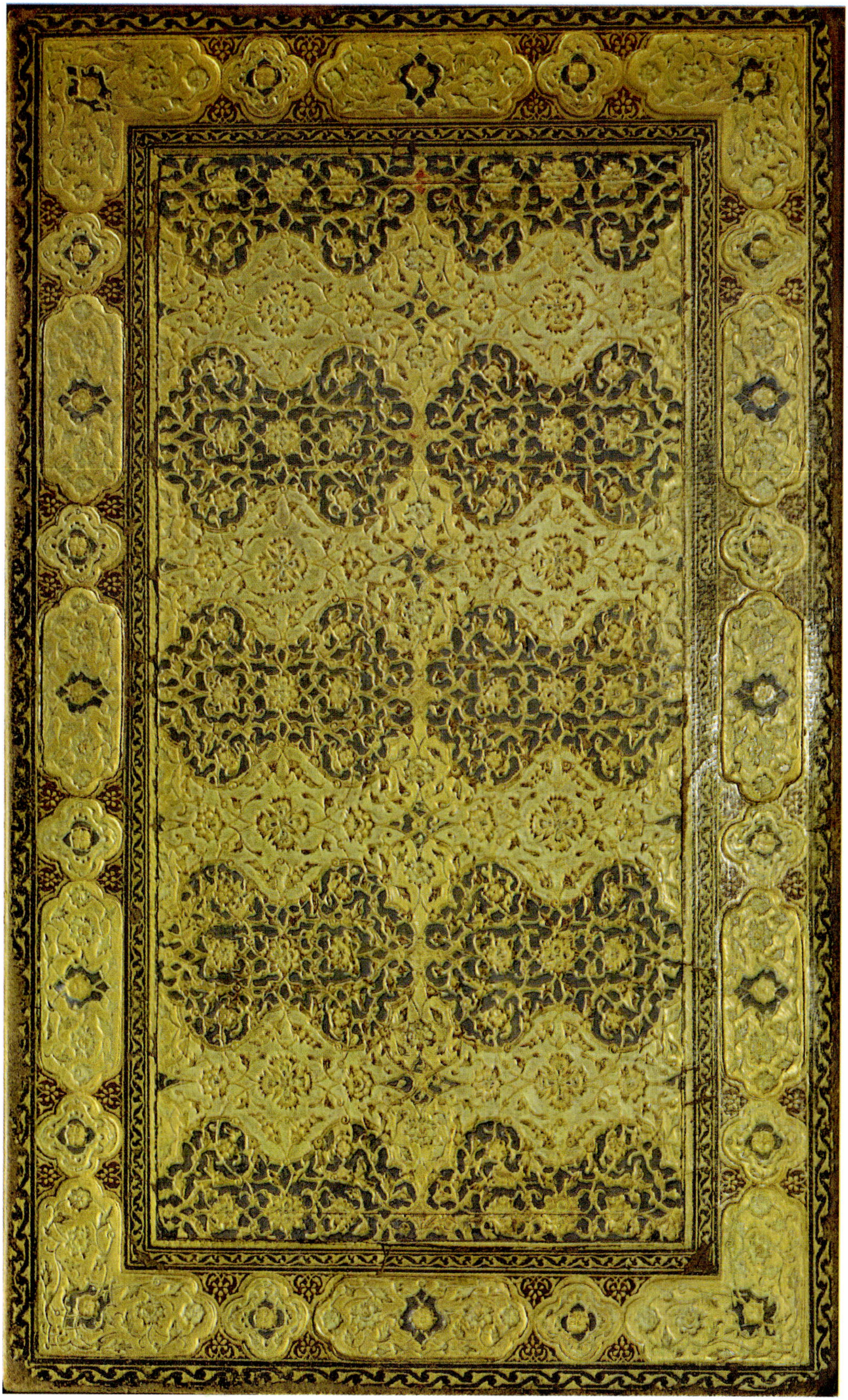

Cover of the *Gulistan* manuscript

Mughal Emperor as their patron Shah Tahmasp gradually became more orthodox and turned away from the art of painting after AD 1544.[23]

The study of the miniatures has been the subject of art historians for considerable time, but the study of the manuscript illumination has evolved in recent years. There are a very large number of illustrated manuscripts now available to us, and with the modern techniques of conservation and preservation, coupled with digitization, it is now possible to access and classify them into broader generic categories for facilitating the understanding of the art of illumination.[24] It includes the comparative study of the first folio, recto and verso (*shamsa, sarluah, 'unwan*), chapter headings, the decoration of text and the borders and the colophon (the last folio).[25]

Banni Singh, Balwant Singh and Mangal Singh were great connoisseurs of art and a large number of paintings and manuscripts were produced under their patronage. They also collected several valuable pieces of art and preserved them in their palaces. Maharaja Banni Singh in particular purchased these valuable specimens of art to set the standard for the artists of his court, who could create works of the highest standard. The contents of the present manuscript are largely based on the AD 1602 version of *Kuliyat-i-Sa'adi* available in the collection of Banni Singh. The binder of this manuscript too is Abdul Rahman, and the volume bearing accession number 206 contains high quality of borders, calligraphy and illumination. Several other copies including one by Agha Mirza of Delhi bearing accession number 601 and comprising two hundred and eighty-five leaves and eighteen illustrations, but incomplete, were also produced during the same period. The quality of the other manuscripts of the period and the illustrations is much lower as compared to the manuscript under study.

Calligraphy, illumination, illustration and binding are the four main elements of the art of book.[26] The Alwar *Gulistan* is remarkable for each of these features. Its miniatures, calligraphy, illumination and binding, are one of the finest examples of the art of the book in India.

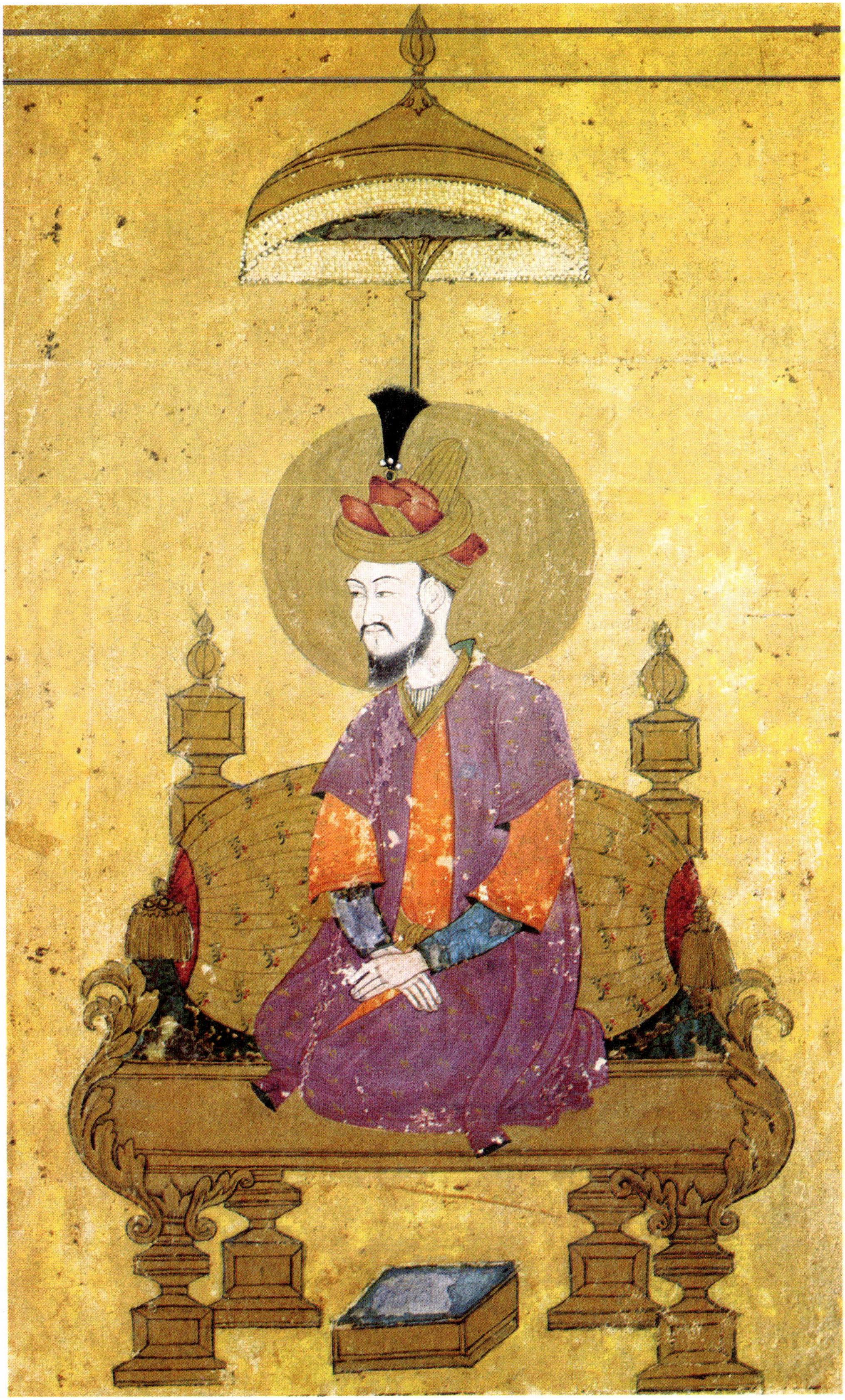

Portrait of Humayun, Murshidabad, c. AD 1765-70 Victoria and Albert Museum

DECORATION OF TEXTS AND BORDERS

THE ART OF preparing illuminated manuscripts evolved over a period of about five hundred years before the present copy of Gulistan was designed. The fourteenth-century Iranian art had already formalized under the school of Shiraz and had attained great heights subsequently under the schools of Herat and Bukhara.[27] The Mughal miniature paintings and the arts of the book borrowed a great deal from the Persian schools in the formative periods and subsequently evolved its own variations. In turn, the regional kingdoms, while emulating the miniature traditions of the Mughal school, maintained some of the salient characteristics *mutatis mutandis*.[28]

The margins or the *hashiya* around the main painting formed an important element of the illuminated manuscripts. During the fifteenth century, in the process of evolution of the margins of the illuminated manuscripts, the artists started using a different paper from the text for the ornamented margins. Filled with floral motifs, landscapes, birds, animals and even human figures at times, the decorated margins came to be known as an integral element of the albums.[29] These elements have also been interspersed between the text in the present manuscript.

The profuse use of the gold and bright yellow tints in the ornamented margins has given both an extra brightness to the page in general and a greater contrast to the main miniature in particular. The floral and geometrical patterns have been used as transparent fillers and are interlaced occasionally with the birds and other symbols. The width of the margin is almost standard throughout the manuscript.

The illumination of the first folio of the manuscript is in the traditional Mughal or Persian style comprising a *shamsa*.

BOOKBINDING

THE ART OF bookbinding was highly developed during the patronage of Maharaja Banni Singh under the professional guidance of Abdul Rahman. Abdul Rahman is said to have learnt the art of bookbinding from a wanderer or *faqir* from Lahore. This is in the traditional Persian style with the block colouring of the board in harmony with the text and the illustrations. The ornamented style of

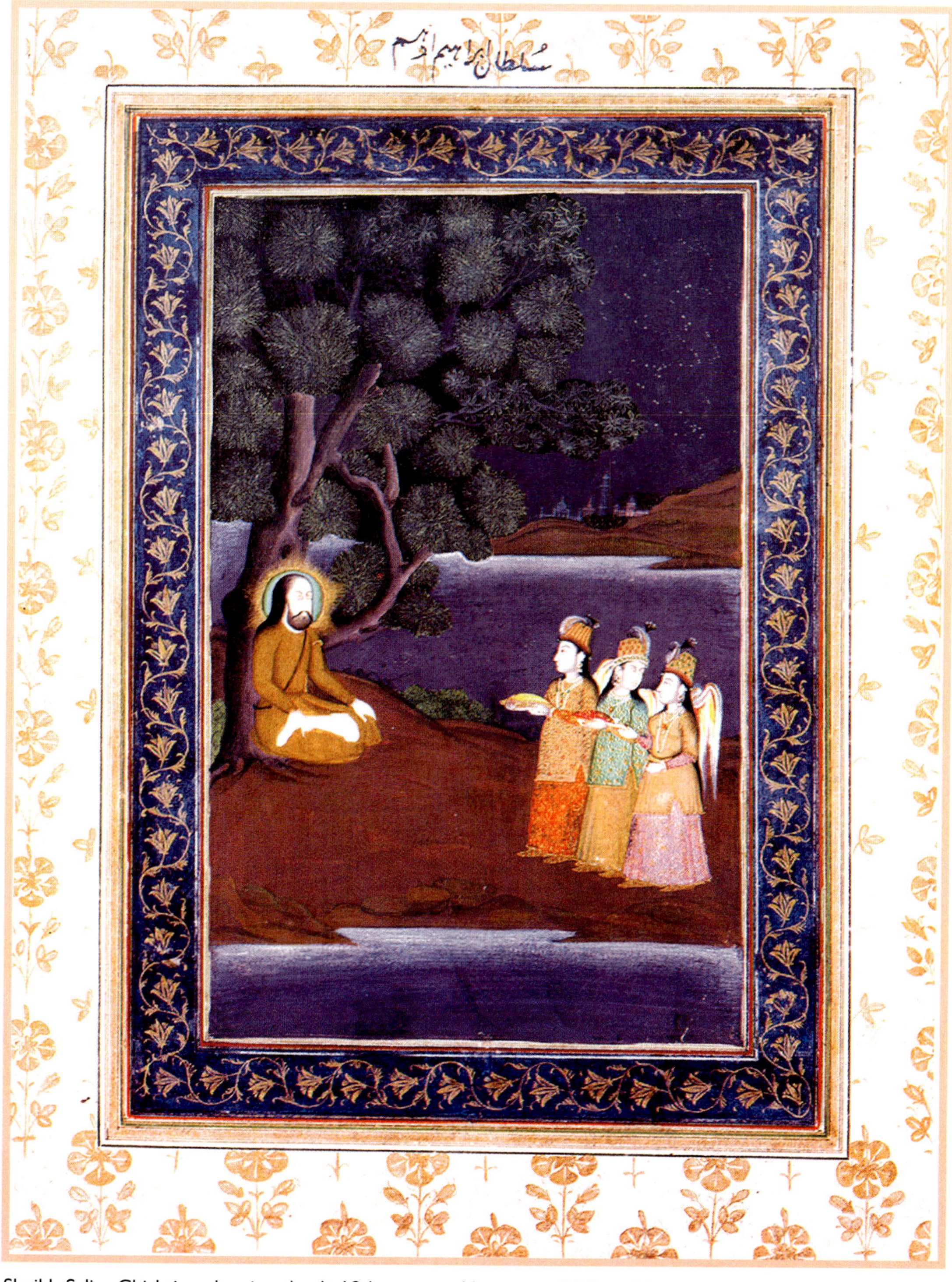

Sheikh Salim Chishti at the river bank, 18th century, Victoria and Albert Museum

bookbinding of the period shows a variety of designs produced by the use of brass blocks. These brass blocks were painstakingly prepared and reused as a permanent instrument changing the patterns, colours and dyes. The painted background was filled with the desired pattern with the brass blocks and then colours were filled with brush in these patterns to give the desired effect. The edges of the books were also coloured with gold or other shades and at times even patterns. The highly professional character of the bookbinding is evidenced from the fact that the use of blocks, colours, patterns, edges and the shades is not only in complete harmony with the main work but is also subordinated to the high quality of the illustrations and the borders inside.

The Gulistan manuscript bears the impact of the most impeccable piece of art. The evidence shows that the team of artists, under royal patronage, was able to produce two pages in a month and the entire illuminated manuscript comprising of two hundred and eighty seven folios took some twelve years to complete.

The manuscript was completed in the year AH 1265 corresponding to the year AD 1856. Ustad Baldeo of Alwar and Ustad Ghulam Ali Khan of Delhi were the master artists for the illustrations, and supervised the team of artists jointly. Contemporary records give the names of some of the important artists of the Kingdom of Alwar as Jamuna Das, Saligram, Chhote Lal, Nanagrama, Rangi Lal, Dalu Ram, Bakas Ram, Balesh Ram, Balaram and Buddha Ram. The head of the team of calligraphist was Agha Mirza of Delhi.

Natha Shah Punjabi and Qazi Abdul Rehman of Alwar designed and illuminated the borders of the text and the miniatures, and the latter also undertook the binding of the work. Each of the medallions of the border took two to four days to complete.

The manuscript comprises seventeen illustrations. The total cost of the entire project, including the wages and salaries of those days, has been estimated at close to over a lakh of rupees.

The size of the folios is thirteen and a half inches by seven inches.[30] Each folio contains eight lines in large *nastaliq* script. All margins have been embellished with gold designs. Colourful medallions with profuse use of gold have been splashed all over the text.

The last illustration is a miniature which shows the completed project being presented by the copyist Agha Mirza to the commissioner, the third chief of Alwar, Maharaja Banni Singh. The Chief Minister or Musahib of the Maharaja, Raja Bahadur Padma Singh is shown seated on the ground. The Darogah Deoriji Lachhman Todamal Baniya, as the head of the porters, is shown introducing the copyist to the Maharaja. Also identified in the illustration are *chairi-bardar* Ladoo Khawas, who is waving the *chamar* or the flywhisk. Standing next to him with the whisk of peacock feathers known as *morchal*, a symbol of rank, is Bal Govind Khawas.

Gulistan has been perhaps one of the most preferred subjects for the artists of the court of Banni Singh. The Museum of Alwar today holds as many as five elaborate copies prepared during the period.[31]

Hendley did the listing and study of the manuscript as early as in AD 1888 and recorded his deep admiration for the work.[32]

NOTES

1 Mohanlal Gupta, *Rajasthan: Zilewar Sanskritik Ewam Aitihasik Adhyayan*, 2 vols., Rajasthani Granthagar, Jodhpur, 2004, vol. II, p. 123.

2 Maharaja Alaghraj, second son of Maharaja Kakil of Amber ruled the area in the eleventh century and his territory extended up to the present city of Alwar. He founded the city of Alpur in 1106 Vikrami Samvat corresponding to AD 1049 after his own name. Later it became Alwar. It was initially spelt as Ulwar but during the reign of Jai Singh the spelling was changed to Alwar.

3 Cunningham has mentioned that Alwar derived its name from the Salva tribe inhabiting the region, and the place was known as Salwapur, a name that changed to Salwar, Halawar and eventually Alwar. Some others hold that the habitation was known as Aravalpur or the city of Aravali named after the hills dividing Rajasthan. Yet some others attribute the name of the city to Alaval Khan Mewati.

4 Deryck O. Lodrick, "Rajasthan as a Region: Myth or Reality", in Karine Schomer, Joan L. Erdman, Deryck O. Lodrick and Lloyd I. Rudolph, eds., *The Idea of Rajasthan: Explorations in Regional Identity*, vol. I, Manohar and American Institute of Indian Studies, Delhi, 2001, p. 17.

5 George A. Grierson, *Linguistic Survey of India*, vol. IX, *Indo Aryan Family, Central Group*, part II, *Specimens of Rajasthani and Gujarati*, Superintendent of Government Printing, Calcutta, 1908.

6 Akbar stayed at the fort of Alwar for a while on way to Fatehpur Sikri in AD 1579.

7 The causes of the "imperial collapse" have been vociferously debated on the wide spectrum ranging from economic exploitation by the rulers and their representatives leading to revolt and uprising on one side to regional assertion as a consequence of economic prosperity on the other. See, Seema Alavi, ed., *The Eighteenth Century in India: Debates in Indian History and Society*, Oxford University Press, Delhi, 2002, p. 2.

8 Muzaffar Alam, "Aspects of Agrarian Uprisings in North India in the Early Eighteenth Century", in Seema Alavi, op. cit., pp. 84-112.

9 C.A. Bayly, *Rulers, Townsmen and Bazaars: North Indian Society in the Age of British Expansion 1770-1870*, Oxford University Press, Delhi, 1992, reprint.

10 Edward S. Haynes, "Patronage for the Arts and the Rise of the Alwar State", in Karine Schomer et al., eds., op. cit., vol. 2, Institutions, p. 205.

11 Edward S. Haynes, 2001, op. cit., p. 267.

12 In the absence of an established law of succession, a minor, Prithvi Singh was raised to the *gaddi* at a tender age of five. The invitation of Prithvi Singh's mother to her father, a non-Kachhwaha, to manage the affairs of the state on behalf of the minor provoked the opposition of the other four leading groups of the royal court, the Nathawats, the Rajawats, the Shekhawats and the Narukas, who started seizing the dominions and refusing to pay the royal dues. M.S. Jain, *Concise History of Modern Rajasthan*, Wishwa Prakashan, New Delhi, 1993, p. 4.

13 Edward S. Haynes, "Imperial Impact on Rajputana: The Case of Alwar 1775-1850", *Modern Asian Studies*, 12, 1978, pp. 419-43.

14 The balancing of the mutually contradictory interests of the chieftains in favour of the new kingdom gave it a character of a feudal state, where the ruler, in the initial years, was at best a *primus inter pares*. For details of the nature and character of feudal polity of the period, see, Alfred C. Lyall, "The Rajput States of India", *Edinburgh Review*, 144, 1876, 1pp. 169-203; Daniel Thorner, "Feudalism in India", *Feudalism in History*, ed. Rushtorn Coulborn, Archon Books, Hamden, 1965; R.P. Vyas, *Role of Nobility in Marwar 1800-1873*, Jain Brothers, Delhi, 1969; Norman P. Ziegler, "Action, Power, and Service in Rajasthani Culture: A Social History of the Rajputs of Middle Period Rajasthan", Ph.D. Dissertation, University of Chicago, 1973; G.D. Sharma, *Rajput Polity: A Study of Politics and Administration of the State of Marwar, 1638-1749*, Manohar, Delhi, 1977; Burton Stein, "The Segmentary State in South Indian History", *Realm and Region in Traditional India*, ed. Richard G. Fox, Duke University Program in Comparative Studies on Southern Asia,

Durham, 1977 and *Peasant, State and Society in Medieval South India,* Oxford University Press, Delhi, 1980; Edward S. Haynes, "A Corinthian Capital on a Column of Ellora: The Transfer of the Concept of Feudalism to the Rajput States of North India", *Journal of Indian History,* 1979, 57, pp. 152-87; Frank Perlin and Burton Stein, "The Character of Old Regime Societies: State Formation and Economy Reconsidered", *Modern Asian Studies,* 1985.

15 Edward S. Haynes, 2001, op. cit., p. 266.

16 "Introduction", *The Idea of Rajasthan,* op. cit., p. xvi.

17 Bakhtawar Singh died without a male child to succeed him. Banni Singh was the son of Bakhtawar Singh's brother Saleh Singh, the *jagirdar* of Thana.

18 Born on 16 September 1808, Banni Singh's major support was from amongst the Rajput nobility of Naruka clan who saw a threat to their pre-eminence in the accession of Balwant Singh. Rajasthan State Archives, Bikaner, S. No., 746, 747; bag 107, collection 4 and 5, pp. 1-4, 5-6.

19 Edward S. Haynes, "Imperial Impact of Rajputana: The Case of Alwar, 1775-1850", *Modern Asian Studies,* 12, 1978, pp. 419-53.

20 Jeremiah P. Lotsy, *The Art of Book in India,* The British Library, London, 1982, p. 5.

21 Ibid., p. 12.

22 Ibid., p. 12.

23 Ibid., p. 75.

24 Oleg F. Akimushkin and Anatol A. Ivanov, "The Art of Illumination", in Basil Gray, general ed., *The Arts of the Book in Central Asia,* Serindia Publications, UNESCO, London, 1979, pp. 35-57, some quarter century back held that "the field is beset with considerable difficulties: the existence of a vast number of illuminated manuscripts scattered all over the world, some still undiscovered", p. 35.

25 Ibid., p. 35. The important systematic studies in this direction include the classical works of I. S. Stchoukine, B.W. Robinson, and R. Ettinghausen.

26 Jeremiah P. Lotsy, op. cit., p. 12.

27 Oleg F. Akimushkin and Anatol A. Ivanov, op. cit., pp. 35-57.

28 Lubor Hajek, *Indian Miniatures of the Mughal School,* London, 1962. Stuart Cory Welch, *Imperial Mughal Painting,* George Braziller, Pennsylvania, 1978; Asoke Kumar Das, *Splendour of Mughal Painting,* Vakils, Feffer and Simons, Bombay, 1986; S.P. Verma, *Painting the Mughal Experience,* Oxford University Press, Delhi, 2005; J.P. Lotsy and

Jeremiah P. Lotsy, *Indian Book Painting*, British Library, London, 1986.

29 Percy Brown, *Indian Painting Under the Mughals*, Hacker Art Books, New York, 1975, p. 91.

30 Lotsy mentions the size as 34.5 x 518 cm. Jeremiah P. Lotsy, op. cit., p. 154.

31 Government of Rajasthan, *Catalogue and Guide to Government Museum, Alwar,* part I, Department of Archaeology and Museums, Jaipur, 1961.

32 Thomas Holbein Hendley, *Ulwar and Its Art Treasures*, W. Griggs, London, 1888.

Sheikh Sa'adi

The Poet and the Mystic

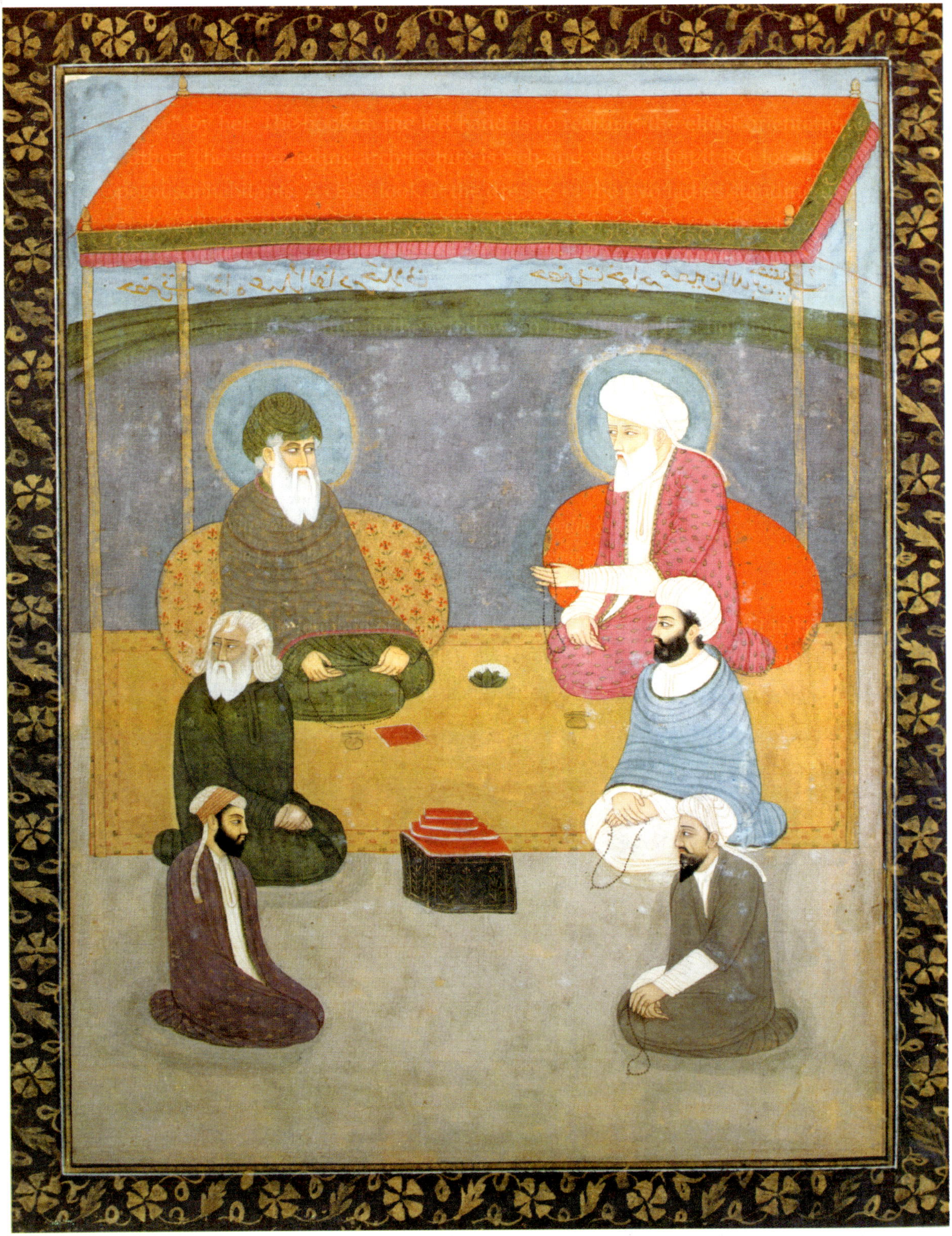

Sheikh Abdul Qadir and Moinuddin Chishti,
Mughal style, *c.* AD 1760-5, Clive Album, Victoria and Albert Museum

SHEIKH SA'ADI, the gem of Shiraz flourished during the most eventful period of the medieval Oriental history, the thirteenth century. Scholars have debated for years about his year of birth and have placed it between AD 1194 and AD 1218. This was the period of the ascendancy of the Mongols and their conquest of Persia, his homeland.

The famous Persian saying "each word of Sa'adi has 72 meanings"[1] epitomizes the profundity of Sa'adi's writings. Mystic schools have claimed him to be one of them; statesmen have held him on the highest pedestal for his learned sayings and littérateurs reckoned him as the *sutut* or pillar of Persian poetry.

Sa'adi was the pen-name of the great scholar, thinker and poet who has been referred to as Musharrif al-Din Muslih al-Shirazi in some of the biographies and by the honorific title of Muslih al-Din in some other.

Gulistan or the Bouquet of Flowers has also been considered as biographical composition. However, this is due to the first person narrative used by Sa'adi, placing himself as a subject of the events and anecdotes.

A famous anecdote refers to a certain friend of the poet fully engrossed with a bunch of flowers in the garden. Sa'adi asked him what was so enchanting about these flowers, which had life for a few days, and most of them would anyway fade before sunset. The friend countered by asking what else in this world could be more entrancing than these flowers. To this, Sa'adi replied that he would compose

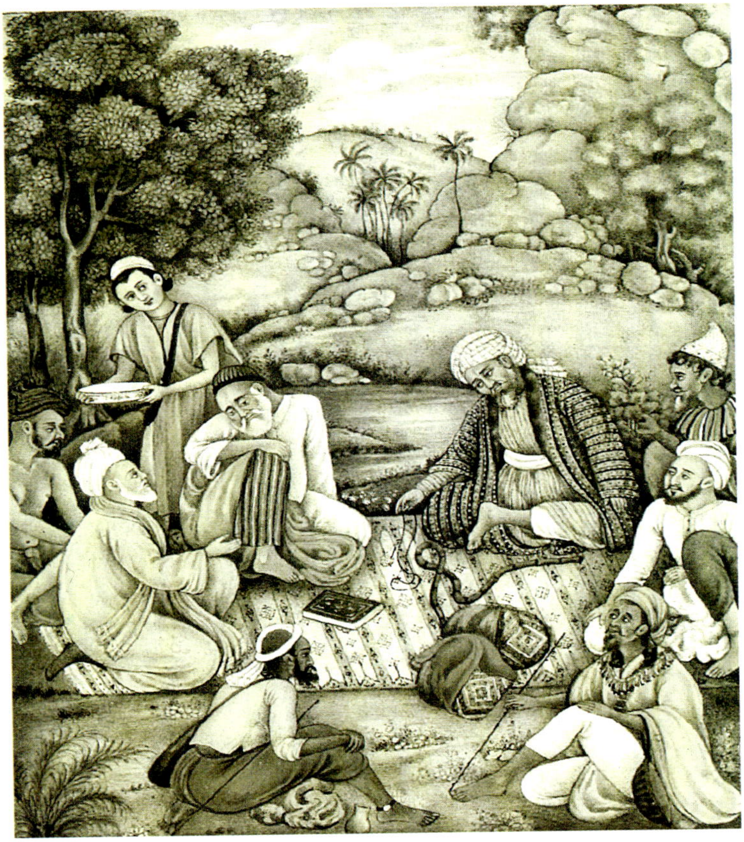

Detail of painting 6

a (book) *Gulistan* that would be not only more captivating than these flowers but would be also far more lasting.[2]

Scholars have divided Sa'adi's life into three parts: the first, from his birth until AD 1226, when he was mostly involved with learning. For the next thirty years or so, he travelled to far-flung places acquiring first hand knowledge and experiences of the cultures around. He finally returned to Shiraz and spent the rest of his life until 1292 contemplating, writing, preaching and guiding people to be righteous.[3]

Gulistan belongs to the genre of Sufi literature.[4] It inspired the post-renaissance Western world significantly, and its Persian couplets were learnt by heart by the colonial officers with great interest to quote and use them to establish their supremacy over the remnants of the native Imperial authority.

American scholars, Thoreau and Emerson have referred to *Gulistan* as a Secular Bible. Byron has called Sa'adi a Persian Catullus.

Sa'adi completed the preface to the compendium in AD 1258, and soon it became a popular treatise among the regality and nobility. Several copies of the work were made by the calligraphers and illustrated by the artists in next centuries that followed and were freely gifted to the counterparts by the emissaries. Thus even India under the Sultans and the Imperial Mughals received a large number of illuminated copies, which are masterpieces of Persian art.

The region of Shiraz enjoyed comparatively undisturbed times and less turbulence due to the Mongol invasions during the thirteenth century. It continued to be a centre of learning, art and culture from the times of Umar Sheikh to Pir Budaq, the two great ends of the Timuride and Turki rulers.[5] When Sa'adi died in AD 1292, Shiraz saw the reopening of the international trade from the Persian Gulf, after a gap of almost two hundred and fifty years.[6] This was followed by the continued patronage to literature under Inju (1342-53) and Muzaffarid (1363-84). All these prolonged favourable vectors contributed to the popularity of the writings of Sa'adi and its export to far-flung areas including India.

Sa'adi was considered to be a benchmark, the standard of excellence and Hafiz called him "the master of lyrical poetry".[7] Ziauddin Barani has referred that Khwaja Hasan Sanjari Dehlevi, the great Persian poet of the thirteenth century, in his lifetime, being conferred upon the honorific title of Sa'adi of Hindustan.[8] Persian language and literature was regarded as a symbol of elitist attainments, and Kaikubad, and later Balban promoted its learning with great zeal. "By the time the Delhi Sultanat was first established, Persia fist had fully evolved as a literary language throughout Central Asia. To take an interest in Persian arts and letters was considered as a mark of refinement and sophistication".[9] Balban's son Prince Muhammad Sultan was an unprecedented supporter of Persian, and while holding the governorship of the province of Multan, he made ambitious plans to raise it to a level of excellence so that it could be recognized as the *Shiraz* of *Hindustan*. For achieving this, he awarded permanent *jagirs*, allocated large sums of funds and successfully convinced his father, Sultan Balban to make large endowments for the maintenance of a seat of learning created in Multan for the purpose of promoting Persian. What is significant to note is that the Prince sent emissaries with invitation to Sheikh Sa'adi twice, requesting him to honour the seat of Multan as its first head or the rector.[10] The name intended to be given to this institution was *khanqah-i Sadiyah*. However, Sa'adi declined the offer on both the occasions on account of his old age and suggested that the void could be better filled by Amir Khusrau,[11] another great poet and his contemporary in India. Khalji and later the Tughluq Sultans patronized Persian literature and many learned men and poets, including great names like Khusrau and Hasan enjoyed state patronage under successive dynasties.[12]

Commenting upon Sa'adi's style,[13] it has been observed that the class of his contemporaneous writings is, "an ode, like a panegyric poem, originated from the

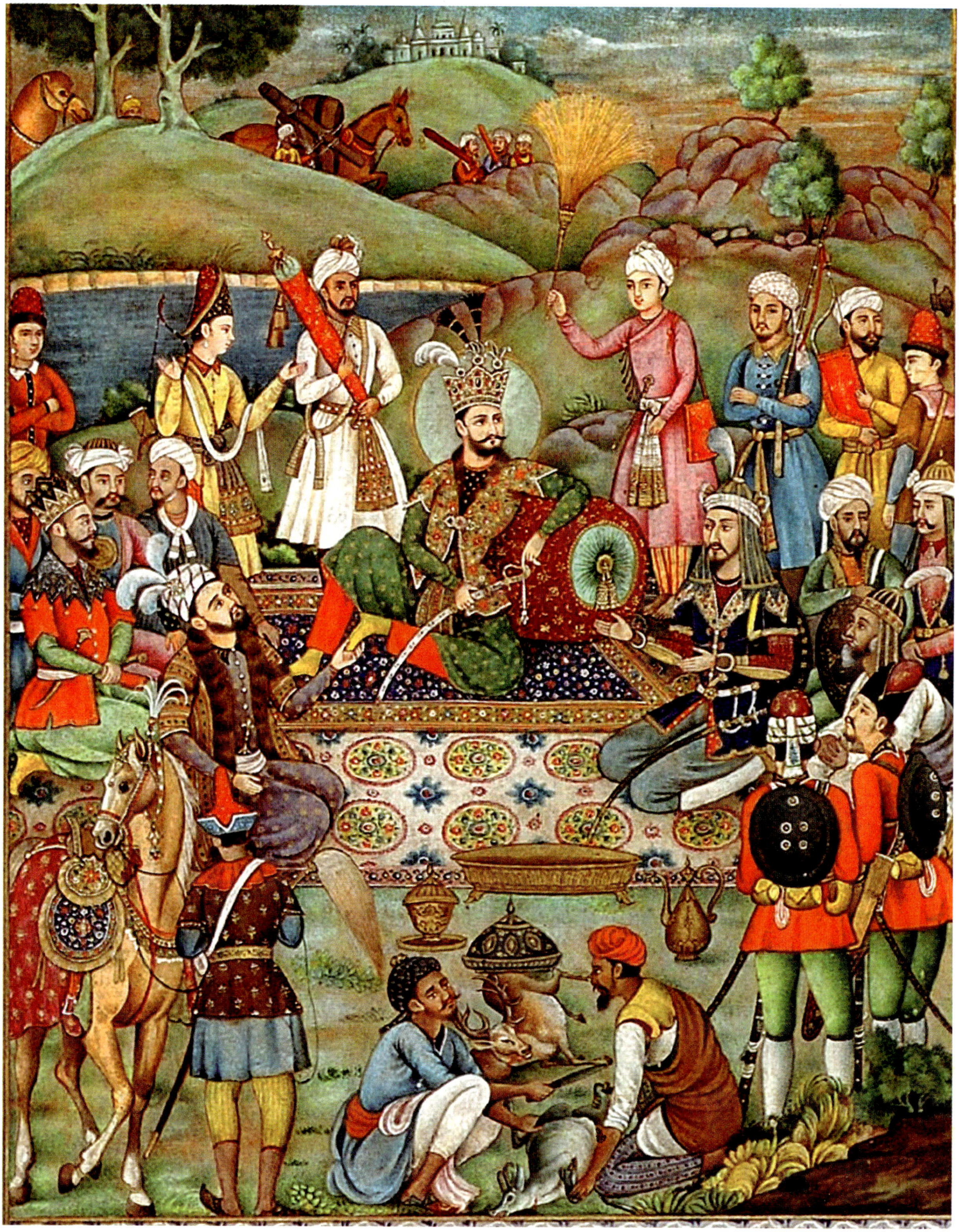

Noushirwan resting during camp. Detail of painting 3

poet's desire to honour some great person or place. Its essential features were the use of refined language and vivid description. Later, it grew more pedantic with a tinge of Sufistic and philosophical thought. The language also became figurative and terse. A lyric, on the other hand, was a tender poem or sonnet composed in simple, sweet and chaste language in praise of one's object of love. It was a love song in which a lover described to his beloved the pangs that he felt or his distraction and the pain of separation that afflicted him so that the beloved might be moved to pity him. But the beloved is depicted to be utterly callous and indifferent to all such wailings, and the reply put in her mouth by the poet is generally that of a proud and unsympathetic party."[14] Scholars have noted the great wit of Sa'adi in several anecdotes,[15] and his writings speak amply of his sharp observations and perceptions.[16]

This phase of Persian literature included many significant elements. "The poets, besides writing an epic, or a love story, or depicting some natural scene of a mountain or river side or a garden in the spring, paid special attention to versifying the common events of the daily life and teaching moral lessons to humanity."[17] Despondency of the time was countered by several inspirational couplets like: Lose not the heart when thy work does not prosper: in a pitch dark cavern lies the Water of Life; or on another occasion, Be pure and fear none O brother: 'tis the unclean cloth which the washer man beats on stones.[18]

The French scholar Andre du Ryer rendered the first known translation of the work in European language as early as AD 1634. In his preface Ryer compared Sa'adi with the uncrowned Prince of Persian and Turkish poetry, and insisted that the Western world should be aware of his profound writings. A German rendering of the selected verses some two decades later followed the French translation. Soon, the Latin and the Dutch translation also became available. Thus, *Gulistan* was exposed to a large cross-section of Western poets, scholars and writers by the seventeenth century.

With the advent of the printing press and the promotion of Persian language among the Company officials the first set of complete works of Sa'adi were published in Persian from Calcutta in 1791-5. However, it was almost one hundred and fifty years after the first French translation that in 1806 the English translation of *Gulistan* by Francis Gladwin could see the light of the day.

French scholars have compared Sa'adi with Jean de La Fontaine (1621-95), whose fables have a striking similarity with the style and message of *Gulistan* and *Bostan*, the two major works of Saadi's.[19]

The moral teachings of Sa'adi inspired the philosophes whose humanitarian and egalitarian writings influenced the French and American revolutionaries during the eighteenth century. Diderot, Voltaire, Hugo, Goethe, Balzac and Ralph W. Emerson have drawn on Sa'adi's sayings to strengthen their views.

NOTES

1 *Har lafz-i Sadi, haftad-o do mani.*

2 His masterpiece writings earned him the status of the uncrowned monarch of *ghazals*. Muhammad Abdul Ghani, *Pre-Mughal Persian in Hindustan*, The Allahabad Law Journal Press, Allahabad, 1941.

3 Sa'adi wrote about a lakh baits, most of which is now extant. Muhammad Abdul Ghani, ibid., p. 419.

4 Muhammad Abdul Ghani, op. cit., p. 325.

5 Basil Gray, "The School of Shiraz", in Basil Gray, gen. ed., *The Arts of the Book in Central Asia*, Serindia Publications, UNESCO, London, 1979, p. 121.

6 N.M. Lowick, "Trade Patterns on the Persian Gulf in the Light of Recent Coin Evidence", in *Near Eastern Numismatics, Iconography, Epigraphy and History: Studies in Honour of George C. Miles*, ed. D.K. Kouymjian, Beirut, 1974, p. 324.

7 Hadi Hasan, *A Golden Treasury of Persian Poetry*, The Publications Division, Ministry of Information and Broadcasting, Government of India, New Delhi, 1966, p. 84.

8 Muhammad Abdul Ghani, op. cit., p. 426.

9 Muzaffar Alam, "The Culture and Politics of Persian in Precolonial Hindustan", in Sheldon Pollock, ed., *Literary Cultures in History: Reconstructions from South Asia*, Oxford University Press, Delhi, 2004, pp. 137-8.

10 "The Prince was so sure of Saadi's arrival in India that he had planned to build a grand *khanqah* with a big college of Persian and Arabic learning attached to it at Multan and to appoint the revered newcomer to be the head of the institution and accord him honour", Muhammad Abdul Ghani, p. 393.

11 Khusrau and his contemporary, Khwajah Hasan were the court poets of Prince Muhammad Sultan for five years. Muhammad Abdul Ghani, op. cit., p. 392.

12 Ahmad Zuhuruddin, "Shuara", in *Tarikh-i Adabiyat-i Musalmanan-i Pakistan wa Hind*, vol. 3, *Farsi Adab I (1000-1526)*, ed. Muhammad Baqar and Vahid Mirza, Punjab University, Lahore, 1971, pp. 207-37; Iqbal Husain, *Early Persian Poets of India*, Patna, 1985, pp. 103-51; Mumtaz Ali Khan, *Some Important Persian Prose Writings of the Thirteenth Century AD in India*, Department of Persian, Aligarh Muslim University, Aligarh, 1970.

13 Sa'adi's pen-name comes from his patron Saad bin Abu Bakr bin Sad bin Zangi, son of the Atabek (viceroy) of Shiraz, Hadi Hasan, op. cit., p. 88.

14 Muhammad Abdul Ghani, op. cit., pp. 128-9.

15 The Shirazis had migrated to Tabriz in such large numbers, mentions Hadi Hasan, that a Tabrizi said to Sa'adi: more than dogs are Shirazis in Tabriz. That is curious, replied Sa'adi, for less than a dog is a Tabrizi in Shiraz, op. cit., p. 84.

16 On contentment, he has challenged the monarchy, while stating that:

If the man of God eats half a loaf, he reserves the other half for the poor;
But if the King swallows a whole country, his earth hunger grows and
he longs for another.

Hadi Hasan, op. cit., p. 93.

17 Muhammad Abdul Ghani, p. 151.

18 Hadi Hasan, op. cit., p. 93.

19 La Fontaine's *Le song d'un habitant du Mogol* is based on a story from *Gulistan* (2: 16).

The Collection

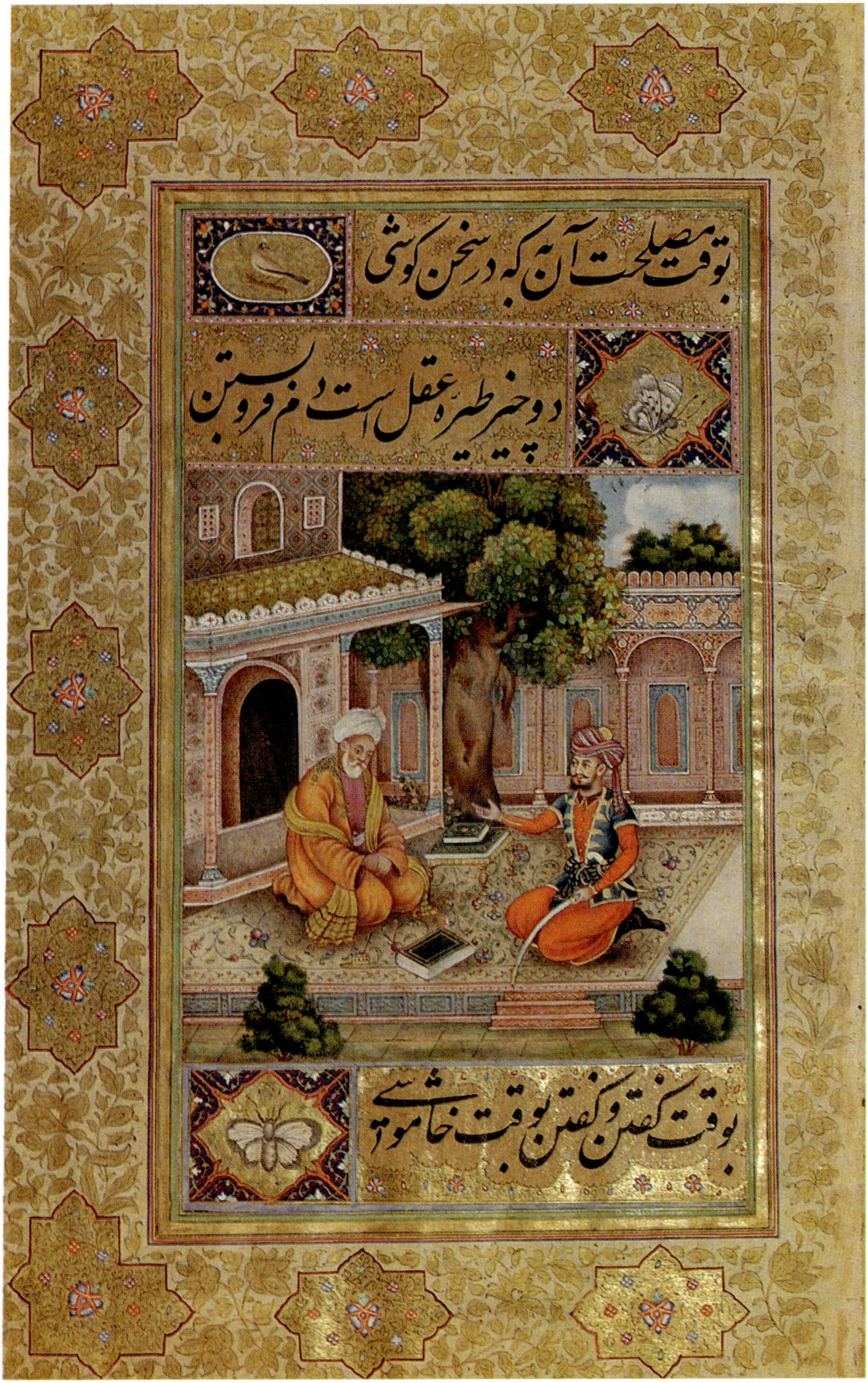
بوقت مصلحت آن به که در سخن کوشی
دو چیز طیرهٔ عقل است دم فرو بستن
بوقت گفتن و گفتن بوقت خاموشی

Painting 1

INSPIRATION FOR COMPOSING *GULISTAN*

THIS IS THE first illustration in the manuscript, added to the introduction of the composition. The introduction comprises two parts. The first part is the traditional invocation or praise to God. The second part of the introduction gives reasons for which the *Gulistan* was written. The inspiration to compose the work was a consequence of a contemplative solitude, when Sa'adi was "reflecting on times gone by"[1] and lamenting fifty years of life he had already wasted in worldly pursuits. Deep contemplation led to his decision to withdraw from society and spend the remaining five days of his life[2] in cleaning his memories of "vain words". To meet this end, he vowed not to "speak idly in future".

No sooner had he became contemplative, withdrawn in solitude, one of his close friends who had travelled with him in a caravan,[3] and had also shared rooms with Sa'adi during rest,[4] entered the room with his usual warmth. However, a similar expected reciprocation from Sa'adi, now after the vow of silence, was missing. Pained at the attitude of the poet, the friend said that one day life anyway would take away the gift of speech; therefore instead of lamenting later, why not speak when the "power of utterance" is still with him.[5]

Responding to the retort of the friend, a servant of Sa'adi's (or perhaps a kinsman) explained to the friend the cause of his silence, and that Sa'adi was determined to pass his remaining life in devotion, without uttering a single word. The friend was also told that if he could not respect Sa'adi's vow, then he must leave instead of forcing him to speak and break his silence.

On hearing to this explanation for the indifferent response of his dear friend Sa'adi, the visitor replied that in regard to their friendship, he would neither leave the place nor move nor even breathe, until Sa'adi had spoken to him with his usual warmth and cheerfulness. He further added that a hastily taken oath may be easily expunged by way of the several prescribed laments like feeding and clothing poor, or setting a captive to freedom or by even fasting for three days. But on the other hand, to keep a friend in agony and suffering is more sinful. Further, exhorting Sa'adi, the friend said that keeping the tongue of Sa'adi encased in his mouth adorning silence is as incorrect as keeping in scabbard *Zu'l-fakar* or the double-edged sword that Prophet Muhammad received from Angel Gabriel and was later owned by his son-in-law, Ali.

Strengthening his argument, the friend said that a tongue in the mouth of mortals is the key that opens the doors to wisdom. As long as "the lid remains shut, how can any person say whether he be a dealer in gems or pedlery?"[6]

In support of the right speech as against absolute silence, Sa'adi then embedded the following moral in the lines that form the theme of this illustration.

INSCRIPTION ON THE PAINTING

Ba waqte maslehat anbakay dar sokhan koshi
Do chiz tiraey aql ast dam pharo bustan
Bawaqte guftan wa guftan bawaqte khamoshi

It has been translated as:

Silence is mannerly, so deem the wise,
But in fitting time use language free;
Blindness of judgment just in two things lies,
Just to speak unwished, not speak unseasonably.[7]

Ross has translated the verse in the following words:

> Though in the estimation of the wise, the silence be mannerly, at the season of giving advice it were better to be explicit. Two circumstances cast a shade over the understanding–that of silence when we should speak, and that of speech when we should be silent.[8]

Gladwin has proposed a more lucid translation:

> Although in the estimation of the wise, silence is commendable, yet at a proper season, free speech is preferable. Two things indicate an obscure understanding; or–to be silent when we ought to converse, and to speak when we should be silent.[9]

The painting depicts the poet sitting in front of his abode in a pensive mood, lamenting and withdrawn and his visiting friend inspiring him to speak and come to his usual cheerful state. The proportion of the house and the trees, both in the foreground and in the background are worth noticing. The two small plants below the plinth inside the courtyard are a unique element, not found usually in the paintings of the Mughal period, where large edifices have been engulfed in the garden.[10] Planting the trees and shrubs inside the courtyard is still very common in today's countryside of Rajasthan.

Another interesting element in the painting is the books, one in front of the poet on a small stool and the other on his right side on the carpet. The binding of the book is almost of the same style as the Gulistan manuscript, and the features have been added to the painting to enhance depiction of intellectual orientation of the characters involved.

The borders of the painting have been embellished with butterflies, on the right side of the top corner and the other on the left bottom. The second upper margin containing a part of the inscription has been enriched by the painting of a fauna. The region even now attracts a very large number of migratory birds who travel from far-off areas for both, resting and nesting. Margins of the painting are exquisitely covered with geometrical and floral designs and motifs. The use of gold in the margins has added to the richness of the work.

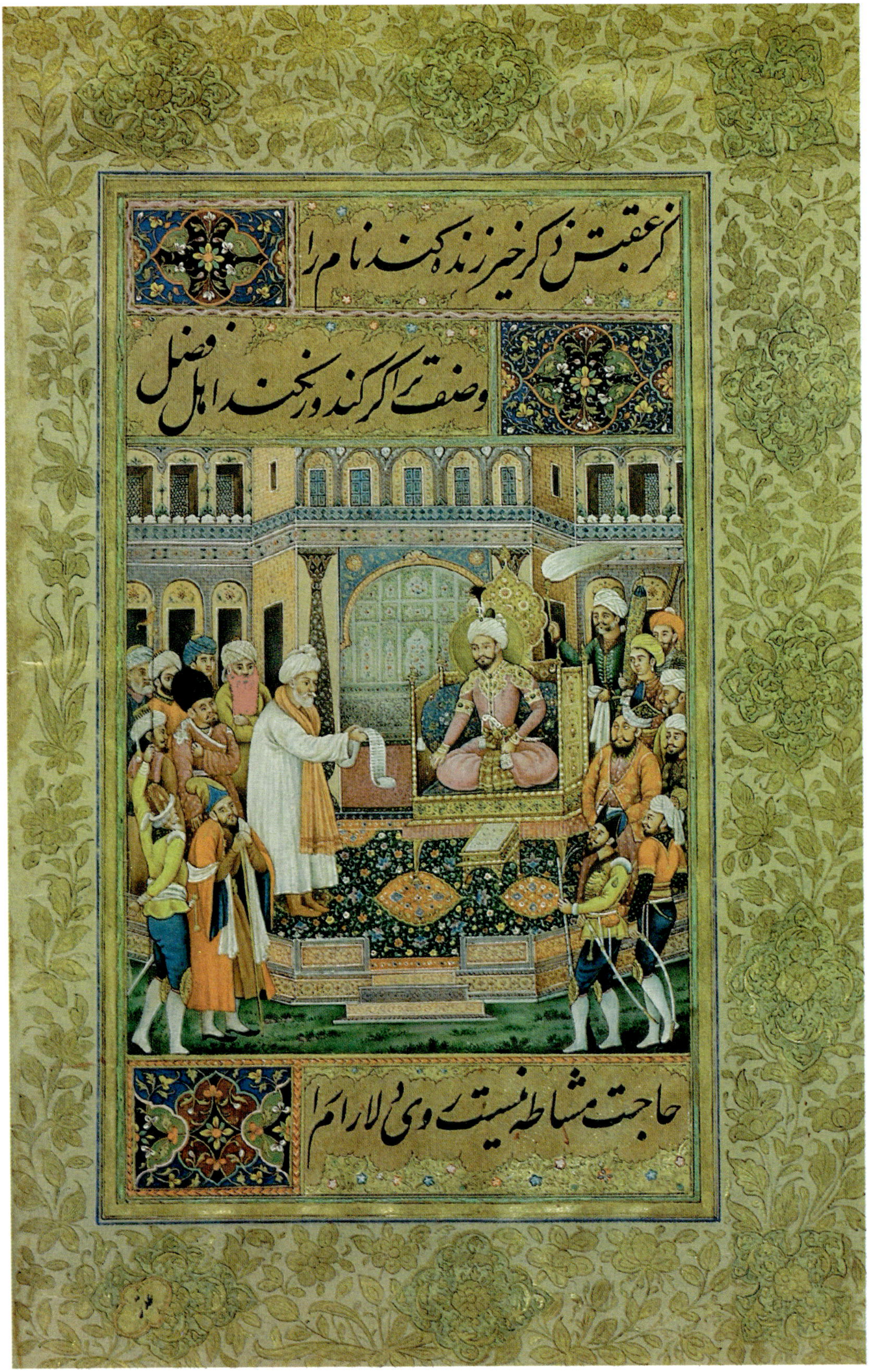
کز عقبش ذکر خیر زنده کند نام را
وصف ترا گر کنند ور نکنند اهل فضل
حاجت مشاطه نیست روی دلارام را

Painting 2

PRESENTING THE *GULISTAN* MANUSCRIPT TO THE KING BY SA'ADI

THE SECOND painting is in continuation of the theme of the first painting, forming that part of the narrative where Sa'adi explains the reasons for composing *Gulistan*. Inspired by the advice of his friend, Sa'adi broke his vow of silence and brought his repentance to an end. He joined his friend in outings in the lap of the beautiful nature, spending time in the night enjoying the moonlight, the stars and the fragrance of the flowers.[11] During one such night both the friends walked in a flower garden, with "fragments of enamel sprinkled on the ground, and the necklace of the Pleiades suspended from the vines that grew there".[12]

After spending a delightful night in the paradisiacal garden, when the two were returning home, Sa'adi noticed a lapful of roses, fragrant herbs and hyacinths, and sweet basil that his friend had picked for himself. On this, Sa'adi remarked that these roses and fragrances are transient, and would fade with time, and that his friend should collect a bouquet that is eternal. On being asked where one could get it, Sa'adi said that he had the gift to compose a *Gulistan* (Garden of Roses) on which "neither the rude storm of autumn shall be able to lay the hand of usurpation . . . nor the revolution of the season convert the serenity of its summer into the gloom of winter".[13]

No sooner than Sa'adi said these words, his friend dropped all the flowers and asked him to immediately compose the Garden of Roses for him as promised.[14] Inspired by the curiosity of his friend, Sa'adi composed two of the chapters of his *Gulistan* over the next few days.[15] In the days that followed and while the roses were still blooming in the garden, the remaining chapters were also composed and the Garden of Roses was complete.

However, the composition, Sa'adi felt would be eternal only when it received the approval and the blessings of the King. "If graced with favour of His Majesty the King, it will become the portrait gallery of China and picture portfolio of Mani; none will, we trust, inspect it with dissatisfaction, for this reason, that a Gulistan, or flower garden, is not the seat of chagrin, more especially as its auspicious preface is inscribed with the name of Saad Abu Bakr Saad bin Zungi".[16]

With the innate desire to seek the approval and blessings of the King on his assiduous composition and immortalize his writing, Sa'adi read out the book in the court, a scene depicted in this painting. Albeit confident of the quality of his composition, his humility did not preclude him to apologize for the shortcomings in the work by citing the example of Buzurchimihr,[17] who was perfect in all respects but used to take a long time to explain himself. When Buzurchimihr came to know about this shortcoming, he said that "It is better to be anxious about what I shall say, than to suffer remorse for what I have said".[18]

For this stamp of approval, Sa'adi presented the composition before the court to the King, in whose praise he wrote several lines in the introductory pages of *Gulistan*. The verse, inscribed on the illustration, has been translated by Ross in the following manner:

> To the crooked back of the sky (or fortune) became straight through joy that she gave a son like thee to the mother of the times. It is a choice instance of wisdom when the benevolence of the Creator selects a servant for the instruction of the people; he obtained immortal fortune whose good fame survived him; for after he is dead the report of his virtue makes his name live forever; it matters not whether the eloquent praise thee or not; for the soul-deluding cheek requires not the tired woman's art.[19]

Eastwick is metrical in translating it as follows:

> For after him, his memory shall by fame endure;
> To thee the praise of learned men nought gives:
> The soul-entrancing cheek needs not the toilette's lure.[20]

Gladwin's translation of the verse is prosaic and straight:

> The sky's incurvated back became straight through delight when dame nature brought forth a son like thee – it is a pure instance of divine mystery when the Creator of the universe out of his benevolence

> distinguishes a servant for the instruction of the mankind. He hath obtained immortality, whose fame liveth, because after his departure the renown of his virtues insures existence to his name. It is matter of indifference, whether the learned praise thee or not, for the face of a beloved mistress requireth not the art of the tire-woman.[21]

The illustration shows Sa'adi reading out his composition in the court before the king. The courtiers and the learned are all listening attentively. The attempt has been to show the dress and the robes of the king, the nobles, and the courtiers to be as contemporaneous to the time it purports as possible, and the throne and the etiquettes of seating follow the pattern close to that of the Mughals, with king seated at the highest level and all the courtiers standing at a designated distance from the Head of the State.[22]

One of the interesting features in this painting is the halo around the monarch. The ideals of kingship in every successive society, irrespective of the religion they followed, have attempted to ordain a status of divinity to the king. The halo around the king in the monarchical traditions of early centuries in South Asia has been very common, and has also been noticed in the earlier traditions of Egypt and Central Asia. However, with the egalitarian emphasis of Islam, it weaned away for some time, until by the third centuries after Prophet Muhammad the nebulous notions of divinity resurfaced. Akbar and consequently his atelier systematically portrayed the king as a divine persona.[23] The regional schools, including Alwar, adopted these techniques as well as emulated these as an accepted format depictions.

INSCRIPTION ON THE PAINTING

Kaz aqbatash zikre khair zindah kunad naam raa
Wasf tora gar kunad war na kunad ahle fazl
Haajate mushaataa niist ruuey dilaaraam raa

. . . he obtained immortal fortune whose good fame survived him; for after he is dead the report of his virtue makes his name live forever; it matters not whether the eloquent praise thee or not; for the soul-deluding cheek requires not the tire woman's art. . . .

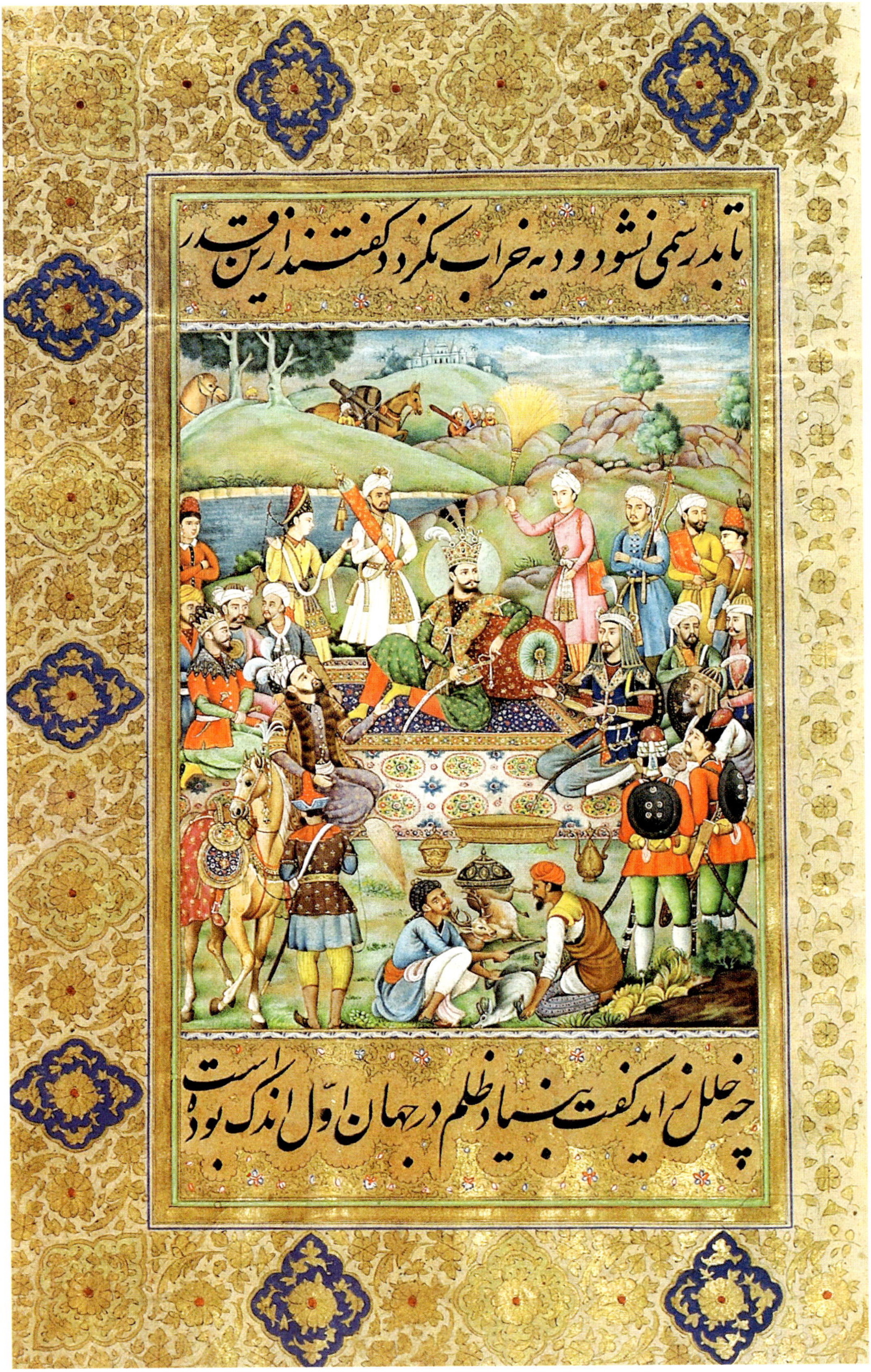

تا بد رسمی نشود و دیه خراب نگردد گفتند ازین قدر
چه خلل زاید گفت بنیاد ظلم در جهان اول اندک بوده است

Painting 3

THE WISDOM OF NOUSHIRWAN

THIRD PAINTING forms the part of the first chapter, entitled "On the Manners of the Kings". The chapter contains forty-one stories setting the high moral standards for the rulers, explaining to them the ideals of a just and benevolent king.

The illustration relates to the nineteenth story, which speaks about the high moral standards set as an example during one of the hunting expeditions of Noushirwan. When the King's entourage settled for rest after a daylong hunting expedition, the cooks mentioned that they did not have salt with them to garnish the roasted meat. It was decided to send a slave to the nearby village to fetch the small quantity required for the evening's cooking. Before the servant could leave, Noushirwan called him and instructed him to pay for the salt that he would fetch from the village, so that extortion, howsoever small, may not ruin the village. The accompanying nobles asked the King how such a small quantity of salt bought without payment could ruin the village. The King answered that the beginning of every injustice in the world has been very small until assuming monstrous proportions.[24]

Ross has translated the event as below:

> They have related that at a hunting seat they were roasting some game for Noushirwan, and as there was no salt they were dispatching a servant to the village to fetch some. Noushirwan called to him, saying, take it at its fair price and not by force, lest a bad precedent be established and the village desolated. They asked

> what damage can ensue from this trifle. He answered, originally the basis of oppression in this world was small, and every newcomer added to it, till it reached to its present extent. Let the monarch eat but one apple from the peasant's orchard, and his guards or slaves will pull up the tree by its root. From the plunder of five eggs, that the King shall sanction, his troops will stick a thousand fowls on their spits.[25]

The illustration shows Noushirwan resting on the couch laid atop a carpet. The halo around Noushirwan is symbolic of the divinity assigned to the monarchical status placed beyond the reach of the commoner and nobility alike. The courtiers and senior military rank holders surround the King. Though appearing to give an impression of a relaxed outdoor setting, the alertness on the face of the bodyguards and attendants adds aura to the ethos. The soldiers are standing at ease in a state of readiness, and the monarch is also holding the sword close to his self.

The cooks and chefs are cleaning and preparing the dishes in close proximity of the monarch and in his clear view. This was one of the Rajput customs while cooking outdoors, to pre-empt any possibility of the poisoning of the food, a common practice during the days of court intrigues. The dishes that have been arrayed include the wash basin for washing the hands, though cooking is at a very preliminary stage.

The royal horse is embellished with several ornamentations, in addition to the protective shields and saddle. The arms of the nobles and soldiers mainly comprise the swords and the bow and arrow. The camel and horse laden with arms and with some soldiers in the far background suggest that some part of the contingent is forming the outer circle for protection.

The vegetation adds to the wilderness of the spot. However, the palace on the far background also depicts the closeness to the urban centre. The design of the carpet is ordinary, and when compared with the designs that appear in other paintings of the collection, it seems that the painters considered the mats, used for outdoor hunting expeditions not so luxurious.

The headgears and the dresses are of a mixed variety, not entirely Persian. They comprise Turkish and European influences, and since the painting is not contemporaneous to the event depicted, such modifications are a natural corollary to the artists' imagination.

INSCRIPTION ON THE PAINTING

Taa badrasmi na shaved wadeh kharaab na gardad guftandazin qadar

. . . lest a bad precedent be established and the village desolated. . . .[26]

Che khalal zayd guft buniyade zulm dar jahaan awwal anadak

. . . what damage can ensue from this trifle. He answered, originally the basis of oppression in this world was small. . . .[27]

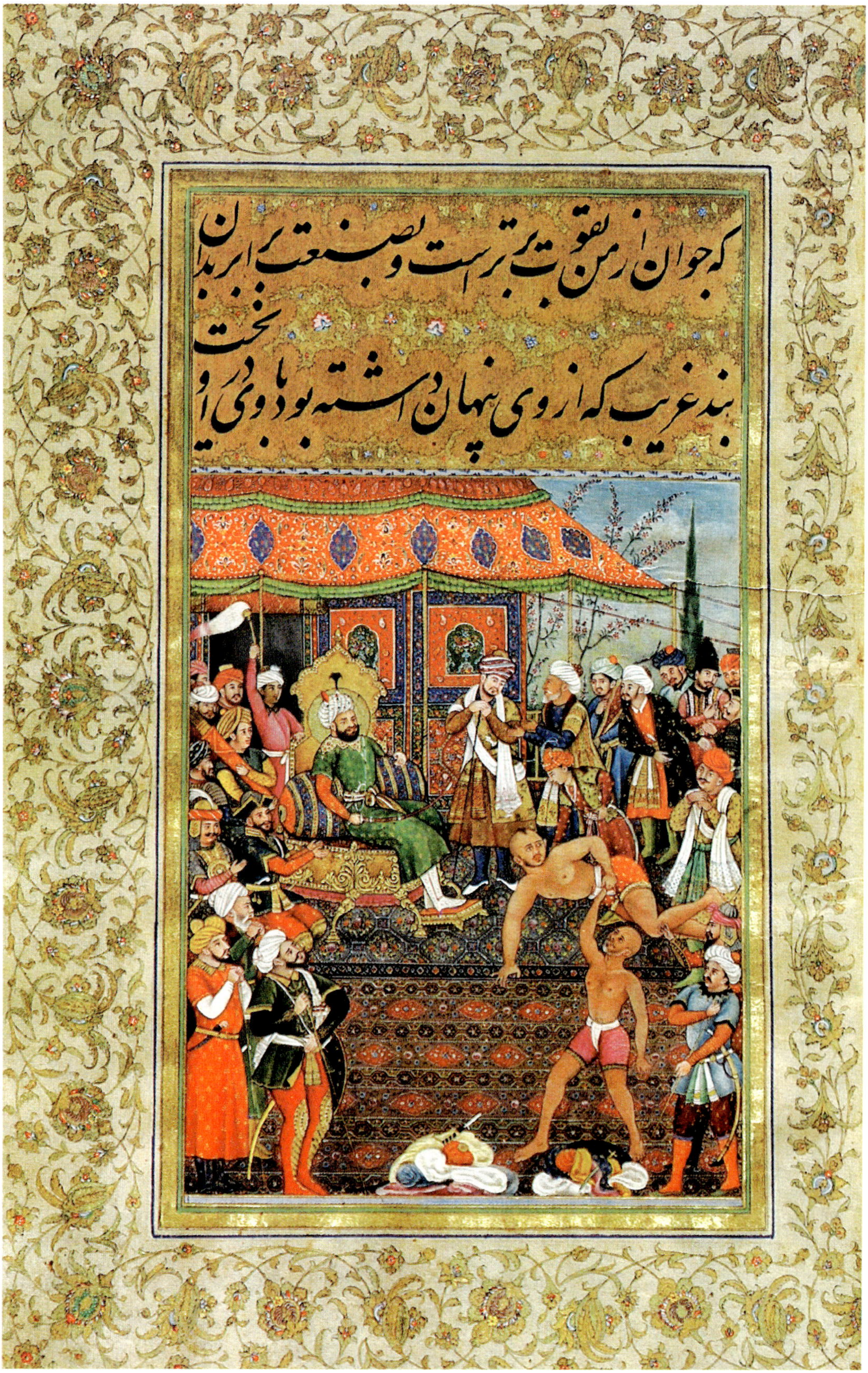

Painting 4

MASTER IS ALWAYS SUPERIOR TO AN ARROGANT DISCIPLE

BOTH, THE fourth and fifth paintings correspond to the story xxvii of chapter I on the Morals of the Kings. It indirectly advises one not to reveal all the secrets of the riches and knowledge even to the most ardent student as it can someday get misused even against one's own self.

Ross has given a simple flowing translation of the story in the following words:[28]

> A person had become a master in the art of wrestling; he knew three hundred and sixty sleights in this art, and could exhibit a fresh trick for every day throughout the year. Perhaps owing to a liking that a corner of his heart took for the handsome person of one of his scholars, he taught him three hundred and fifty of those feats but he was putting off the instruction of one, and under some pretence, deferring it.[29]
>
> In short the youth became such a proficient in the art and talent of wrestling that none of his contemporaries had ability to cope with him, till he at length had one day boasted before the reigning sovereign, saying, to any superiority my master possesses over me, he is beholden to my reverence of his seniority, and in virtue of his tutorage; otherwise I am not inferior in power, and am his equal in skill. This want of respect displeased the King. He ordered a wrestling match to be held, and a spacious field to be fenced in for the occasion. The ministers of state, nobles of the court, and gallant men of the realm were

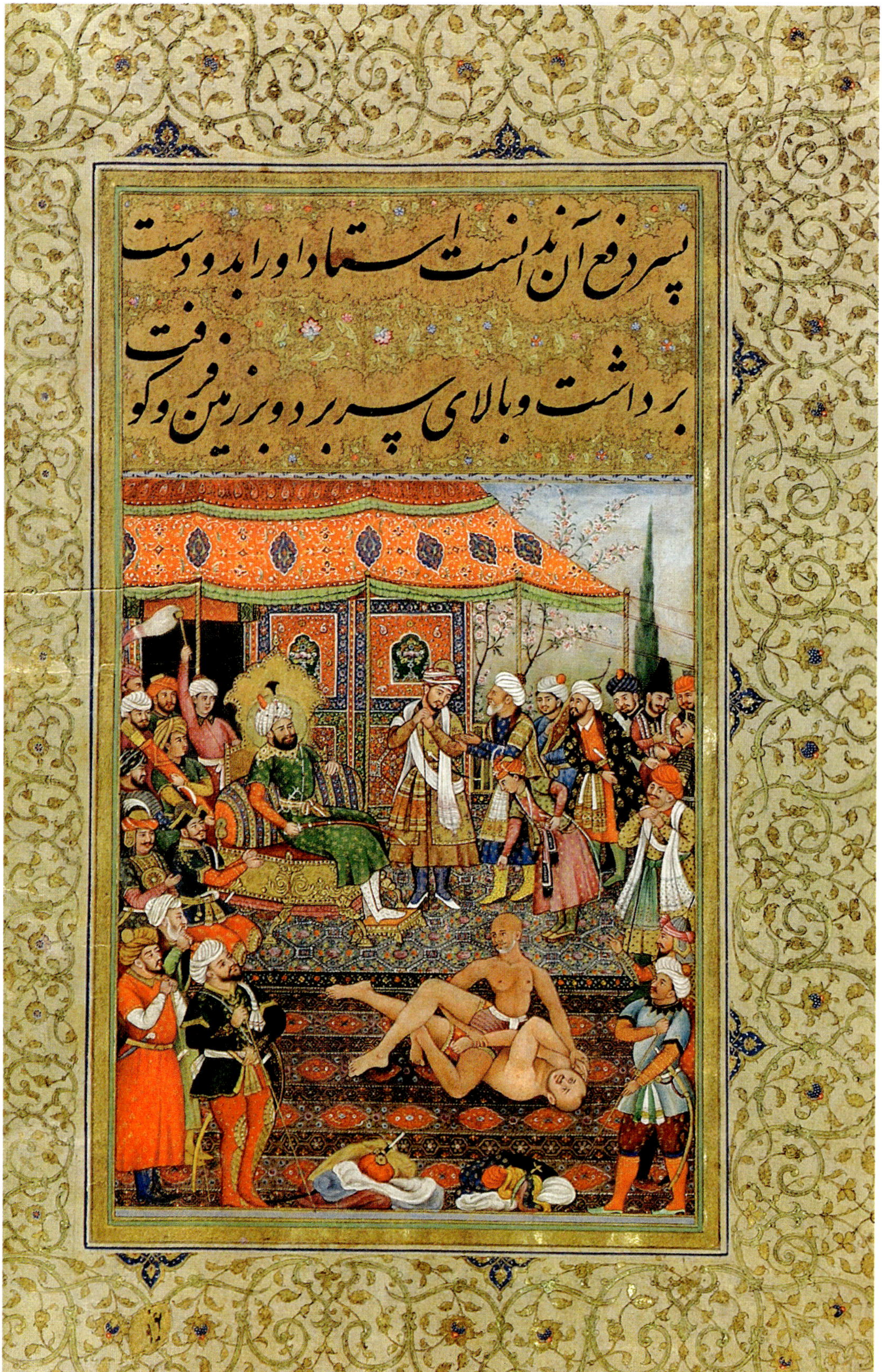
پسر دفع آن ندانست استاد او را بدو دست
برداشت و بالای سر برد و بر زمین و کوفت

Painting 5

assembled, and the ceremonials of the combat marshalled. Like a huge and lusty elephant, the youth rushed into the ring with such a crash that had a brazen mountain[30] opposed him he would have moved it from the base.

The master being aware that the youth was his superior engaged him in that strange feat of which he had kept him ignorant. The youth was unacquainted with its guard. Advancing, nevertheless, the master seized him with both hands and, lifting him bodily from the ground, raised him above his head and flung him on the earth. The crowd set up a shout. The King ordered them to give the master an honorary dress and handsome largess, and the youth he addressed with reproach and asperity, saying, you played the traitor with your own patron, and failed in your presumption of opposing him.[31] He replied, O Sire! My master did not overcome me by strength and ability, but one cunning trick in the art of wrestling was left which he was reserved in teaching me, and by that little feat had today the upper hand on me. The master said, I reserved myself for such a day as this. As the wise have told us, put it not so much into a friend's power that, if hostilely disposed, he can do you an injury. Have you not heard what that man said who was treacherously dealt with by his own pupil: either in fact there was no good faith in this world or nobody has perhaps practised it in our days; no person learned the art of archery from me who did not in the end make me his butt.[32]

The fourth painting shows the wrestling ring, with the monarch seated in the central position in the viewers' gallery. The halo around the monarch is the usual distinguishing feature assigning him the highest status at par with divinity. The nobles, courtiers and the soldiers are standing according to their hierarchy. The throne is made of gold and the backrest and footrest show the special comforts imparted to the monarch. His headgear adorns precious stones studded in harmony with the other ornaments.

That the arena has been specially designed for the occasion is evident from the fact that a temporary tent-like structure is erected in the background. Colourful in design and decoration, the structure is meant to provide shade for the monarch and also being a place to take rest.

The treatment of the subject of amazement on the faces of the King and the courtiers while the master has raised the boastful student with the secret sleight that he was not taught has been handled remarkably by the artist. Similarly, the relative depiction of the age, virility and maturity between the master and the student has been dealt with great finesse. The clothes of the two contestants are lying on the floor, including the dagger and the headgear. The astonishment on the face of the student in the first painting and the helplessness while he has been floored in the second painting is noticeable.

While the majority of the viewers are applauding in both the paintings, the King is more composed befitting his stature. In the second painting, the left hand of the King resting on the pillow has moved a little showing his involvement with the event beyond being a mere spectator.

The carpets, both under the throne and the one used for the arena are spectacular in design and richness. The shade used for the tent is bright and imparts richness to the painting. The most delicate treatment is of the flowering tree behind the tent, with pink, red and green colours used in a rhythmic combination. The dresses of the monarch, nobles, courtiers, and the attendants reveal a great deal about the sartorial habits of the Persian courts as viewed by the contemporary regional artists. The relative richness of the adornments conveys the hierarchy of the individuals. The postures of the two guards standing in the foreground with long sticks in their hands matches well with the body language of each and every viewer in the painting, and their gestures give a dynamic feel to the ethos. While applauding the success of the master, in both the paintings, some are addressing the King and some are talking to themselves, while the remaining are awestruck.

The fifth painting is a continuation of the fourth and has minor variations. For example, it is different in terms of the blossom on the trees and the shades of the sky in the background, that too if seen minutely. However, such variations can take place because of both, the drawing being rendered by a different team, or a significant gap between the completion of the first painting and the start of the second painting, by which time the perceptions of the same set of artists could also change. Nevertheless, the borders and margins of both the paintings are significantly different in style, which is intentional. Another minor difference is seen in the head of the stiletto of the monarch tucked to his belt around his waist.

Interestingly, the shade of the garments of the master in the second painting is totally different. There are similar minor variations in the dresses of the nobles and the courtiers.

INSCRIPTIONS ON THE PAINTING

Painting No. 4

Ke jawan az man bequwate bastar ast wa basan'at baraabar bidaan
Bande gharib ke ajube pinha na daashta buud baawaye dar aawekhta

. . . The master being aware that the youth was his superior engaged him in that strange feat of which he had kept him ignorant. . . . [33]

Painting No. 5

Pesrey dafa aan nadaanist ustaad uraa bado dast
Bardaasht wa baalaaye sipar berad wa bar zamiin faro koft

. . . The youth was unacquainted with its guard. Advancing, nevertheless, the master seized him with both hands and, lifting him bodily from the ground, raised him above his head and flung him on the earth. . . . [34]

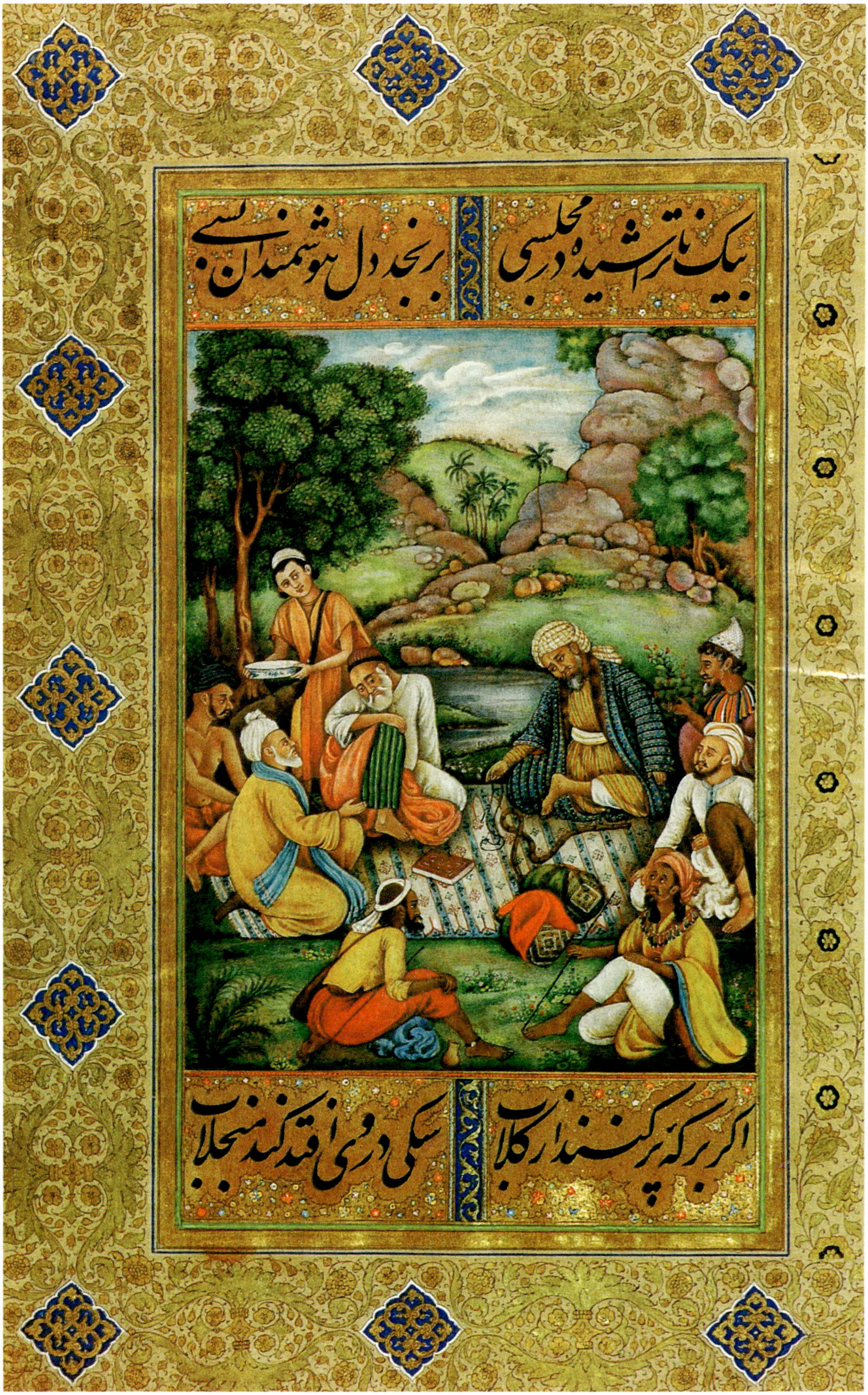
بیک ناتراشیده در مجلسی
برنجد دل هوشمندان بسی
اگر برکه پرکنند از گلاب
سگی در وی افتد کند منجلاب

Painting 6

SEEKING THE COMPANY OF DARWESHES

THE SIXTH PAINTING shows the narration translated by Ross as story v of chapter II as below:[35]

> Some travelling mendicants had agreed to club in a body and participate in the cares and comforts of society. I expressed a wish that I might be one of the parties, but they refused to admit me. I said: It is rare and inconsistent with the generous dispositions of darweshes to turn their faces from a good-fellowship with the poor, and to deny them its benefits, for on my part I feel such a zeal and good-will, that in the service of the liberal I am likely to prove rather an active associate than a grievous load. "Though not one of those who are mounted on the camels, I will do my best, that I may carry their saddle-cloths."[36]
>
> One of them answered and said: Be not offended at what you have heard, for some days back a thief joined us in the garb of a darwesh, and strung himself upon the cord of our acquaintance. "How can people know what he is that wears that dress. The writer can alone tell the contents of the letter." In consequence of that reverence in which the darwesh character is held, they did not think of his proligacy, and admitted him into their society. "The outward character of the holy is a patched cloak; this much is sufficient, that it has a threadbare hood. Be industrious in thy calling, and wear whatever dress thou choosest. Put a diadem on thy head, and bear a standard on thy shoulder. Holiness does not consist in a coarse frock. Let a zahid, or holy man, be truly pious, and he may dress in satin. Sanctity is not merely a change

of dress; it is an abandonment of the world, its pomp and vanity. It requires a hero to wear a coat of mail, for what would it profit to dress an hermaphrodite, or coward, in a suit of armour?"[37]

In short we had one day travelled till dark, and at night composed ourselves for sleep under the wall of a castle. That graceless thief took up his neighbour's ewer, saying, I am going to my ablutions; and he was setting out for plunder.[38] "Behold a religious man, who threw a patched cloak over his shoulders; he made the covering of the Cabah the housing of an ass."[39] So soon as he got out of the sight of the darweshes, he scaled a bastion of the fort and stole a casket. Before break of day that gloomy-minded robber had got a great way off, and left his innocent companions asleep. In the morning they were all carried into the citadel, and thrown into a dungeon. From that time we have declined any addition to our party, and kept apart to ourselves, for there is safety in unity, but danger in duality or a multitude. "When an individual of a sect committed an act of folly, the high and the low sunk in their dignity. Dost thou not see that one ox in a pasturage will cast a slur upon all the oxen of the village?"[40]

I said: Let there be thanksgiving to a Deity of majesty and glory that I am not forbid the benefits of darweshes, notwithstanding I am in appearance excluded from their society; and I am instructed by this narration, and others like me may profit by its moral during their remaining lives. "From one indiscreet person in an assembly a host of the prudent may get hurt. If they fill cistern to the brim with rose-water, and let a dog fall into it, the whole will be contaminated."

The painting shows Sheikh Sa'adi in the company of darweshes in the wilderness of a mountainous region, requesting them to allow him their company. The greenery and vegetation invokes both hermitage and prosperity, and the dresses chosen for the group by the artists have been carefully selected. The leader is fully dressed with the headgear and the shawl, though by appearance the clothes are coarse and dull in shades. The other members of the group are also dressed in non-expensive but complete attire. However, only one of the members of the group, sitting behind Saadi, is not wearing the clothes on the upper part of the body, and the comfortable composure on his face gives an impression that he is used to being scantily dressed. His presence also adds to the ethos of renunciation surrounding the company of the darweshes.

A young man carrying a dish and listening to the conversation while moving in another direction suggests that the preparations for the meals are on. Then small sticks in the hands of the two members sitting in the foreground are the only protection the group has. Their belongings are not much except for two bundles stacked on the carpet.

A book has been added to the gathering lying on the carpet to emphasize the elitist character of the learned gathering. The leader of the group is holding a band of beads and somewhat-immersed in the chants, with the saint sitting next to him in a white shirt is very meditative, with scant concern with the ongoing conversation. Every individual member of the group is sombre, composed, and serene.

The posture and body language of Sa'adi is a mix of importunate persuasion, and making his point why he should not be deprived of the pleasure of their mutually beneficial company. Curiously enough, though set in the outdoors, the scene does not have any fauna or other living creatures.

INSCRIPTIONS ON THE PAINTING

Bayak na tarashiida dar majalisey be sajad diley hoshmandan basey
Agar bar kahe pur kunanda azgulaab sagey dakhey uftad kunad munjilaab

. . . from one indiscreet person in an assembly a host of the prudent may get hurt. If they fill the cistern to the brim with rose-water, and let a dog fall into it, the whole will be contaminated. . . .[41]

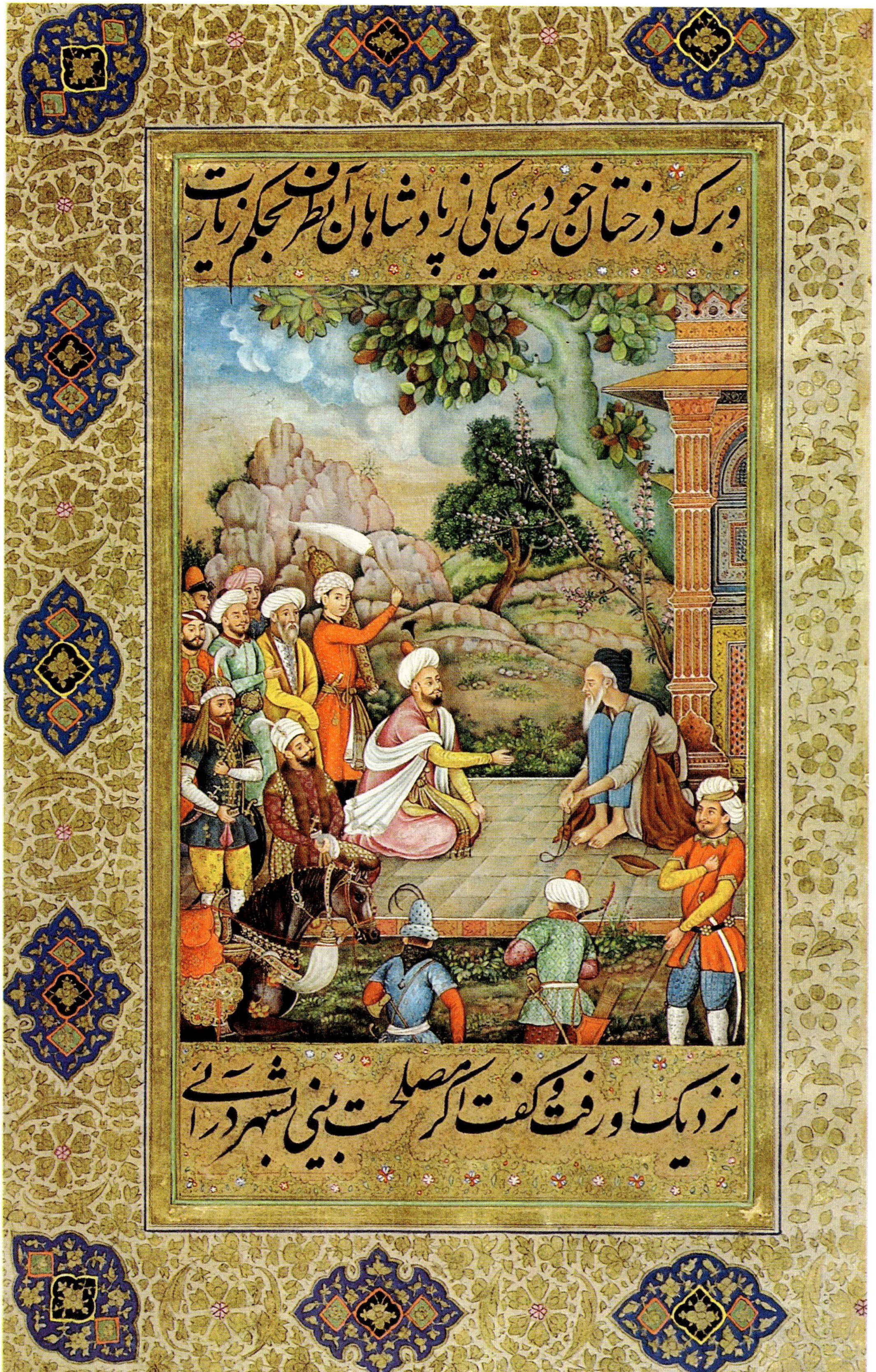
و برگ درختان خوردی یکی از پادشاهان آن طرف بتجمل زیارت
نزدیک او رفت و گفت اگر مصلحت بینی بشهر درآئی

Painting 7

THE DARWESH IN THE WORLDLY COMFORTS

THE SEVENTH and eighth paintings are related to the stories translated by Ross in chapter II, as story xxxiii in the following words:[42]

> One of the holy men of Syria had passed many years of devotion in the wilderness, and was feeding on the leaves of trees.[43] The king of that country, in the way of a pilgrimage, visited him, and said, If you can see the propriety of removing into my capital I will prepare an abode,[44] where you may perform your devotions more at ease than in this place, and others may benefit by the blessing of your spiritual communion, and be edified by the example of your pious labours. The hermit was adverse to this advice, and turned away his face. One of the king's ministers spoke to him, saying: For the satisfaction of his majesty, it were proper that you would for a few days remove into the city, and ascertain the nature of the place: when, if it should prove that your purity might be tarnished by coming in contact with the wicked, you have still the option left of moving back.[45]
>
> It is reported that they prevailed on the hermit to accompany them into the city; and, in a garden near the sacred residence of the king, prepared for him a dwelling, which, like the mansions of paradise, was rejoicing the heart, and exhilarating the soul[46] — "Its damask roses were blooming as the cheeks of the lovely, and its tufted spikenard like the ringlets of our mistresses. It had as much to fear from the angry blasts of winter as the babe who has not yet tasted its nurse's milk:[47] boughs of trees on which hung crimson flowers that gleamed like a flame amidst their dusky foliage."[48]

Forthwith the king sent him a moon-faced damsel. "Such was this delicate crescent of the moon, and fascination of the holy, this form of an angel, and decoration of a peacock, that let them once behold her, and continence must cease to exist in the constitutions of the chaste."[49]

And, in like manner, there followed her a youth of such rare beauty and exquisite symmetry, that the powerful grasp of his charms had broken the wrists of the pious, and tied up behind their backs the arms of the upright[50] "Mankind stand — around him parched with thirst, whilst he, who seems thy cup-bearer, will give thee no drink. The eye could not be satiated by beholding him, like the dropsical man with water by looking at the river Euphrates."[51]

The hermit began to relish dainty food, and to wear sumptuous apparel; to regale himself with fruits, perfumes, and sweetmeats; and to behold with delight the charms of the handmaid and bondsman. And the wise have said — The ringlets of the lovely are a chain on the feet of reason, and a snare for the bird of wisdom.[52] "To the mystery of thy service I devoted my heart, religion, and all my mental faculties;[53] verily, I am now the bird of reason, and thou art the lure and bait."[54]

In short, the good fortune of his many years of sanctity ran to waste, as has been said "Whatever he had laid up from theologician, sage, or saint, or of recondite knowledge from the eloquent and pure of spirit, now that he had stooped to mix with a vile world like the foot of a fly he got entangled in its honey."[55]

The king had the curiosity of making him another visit, and found the hermit much altered from what he first saw of him. His face had become fair and ruddy, and his body plump and jolly; and he was reclining at his ease on cushions of brocade,[56] and had the Hoori-like damsel lolling by his side, and the fairy-formed youth holding a fly-flap of peacock's feathers in his hand, and standing by him in attendance. The king congratulated him upon his portly appearance, and they entered together upon a variety of topics, till his majesty concluded by observing, in this world I have affection for these two orders of mankind, the learned and the recluse.[57] A philosophic vizier, and man of much worldly experience, happened to be present. He said: O sire! Such is the canon of affection that you should confer a benefit on each. Give money to the learned man, that he may teach others; and give nothing to the hermit, that he may remain an anchorite. "A zahid, or hermit, stands in need of neither diram nor dinar; when an anchorite takes either, look out for another.[58] Whoever is virtuously disposed, and holds a mystical communication with God, is sufficient of a hermit without requiring the bread of charity, or the crumbs of mendicity.[59] The tapering finger of the lovely, and her soul-deluding earlobe, are decoration enough without a turquoise ring or ear-jewel.[60] Tell that piously-disposed and serene-minded darwesh that he needs not the bread of consecration or scraping of beggary;[61] tell that handsome and fair-faced matron that she does not require paint, colouring, or jewellry.[62] When I have of my own, and covet what is another's, if they esteem me not a hermit they treat me as I merit."[63]

The complete narration of the event is covered in two paintings remarkably fine and rich in presentation. The seventh painting shows the monarch visiting the hermit in the "wilderness" of his deprivation. The part of the structure where the hermit has been shown living in this painting, somehow gives an impression that the place chosen by him to live was perhaps lacking food and other comforts but not the shelter. The edifice shown is well-structured and strong built, with red-sandstone filigree and painted doors.

The painting shows the king with his entourage on one side and the hermit on the other, while he is attempting to convince the saint to agree to the suggestion of moving to the comforts of his palace. The saint is holding the beads in his clamp, is withdrawn inwards and an empty bowl lying next to him adds to the frugal nature of his belongings. His appearance is frail and clothes sufficient but frugal. There is no carpet and even the monarch is sitting on the bare floor. His richly decorated horse is in the foreground and the bodyguards and other attendants in a state of alert. The trees in the background are blossoming and some birds in the far-left corner have been added to enhance the feel of the natural surroundings far from the urban centre. There is no other edifice visible in the scene emphasizing the isolation of the dwelling. The king, supported by his group is persuasive while the hermit is contemplative of his suggestion, yet to make up his mind.

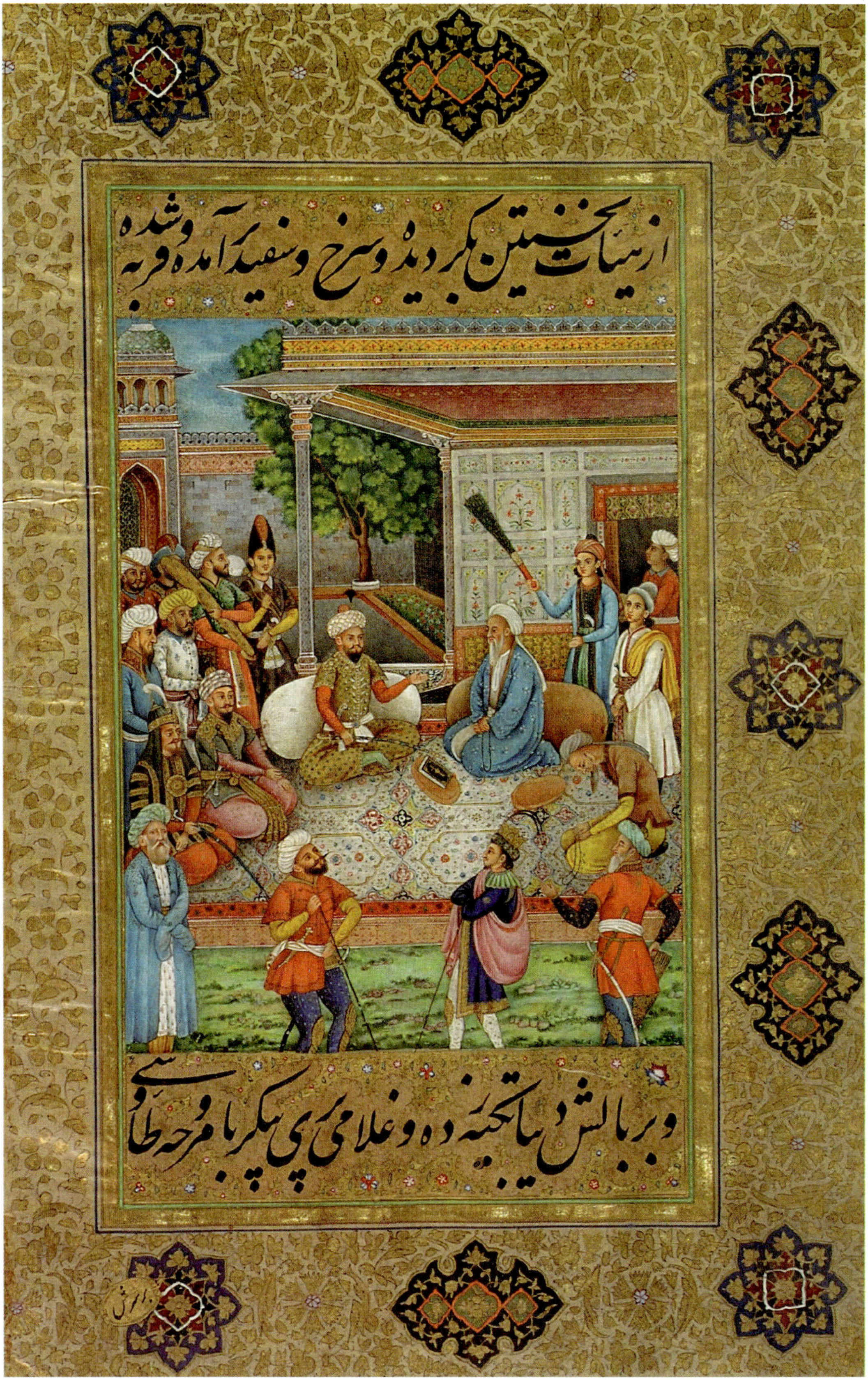
ازینسان نخستین نکر دیده و سرخ و سفید آمده فربه و شده
و بر بالش دیبا تکیه زده و غلامی پیکر با قرطه طاوسی

Painting 8

The eighth painting shows the rich surroundings of the palace with maids standing in service behind the hermit who is now richly dressed and has also become somewhat stout and still holding the beads in his hands, but with a book before him. The exquisitely painted walls of the palace, the well structured edifice and the rich carpet on which the visiting monarch and his accompanying nobles are sitting is a great contrast to the earlier dwelling unit of the hermit that he had abandoned on the suggestion of the king to move into the royal comforts of urban life. The courtiers and the attendants are all listening to the curious conversation between the monarch and the hermit.

The courtyard in the background has blossoming parterres with colourful flowers. The marble inlays and pietra dura on the walls behind the hermit adds to the luxurious surroundings the artists have attempted to depict. The dress, the headgear and the sitting posture of the hermit when compared with the first painting, show a significant change befitting his metamorphosis in the lavish and opulent ethos of the palace. The maids attending to him in the background are subdued and attentive to the conversations, like the other courtiers. The dress of the attendants and bodyguards in the foreground has an European influence. A senior citizen, in the foreground with a blue gown and a concerned look on the face adds to the seriousness of the occasion. The addition of a saintly figure engrossed with beads and head hung down in a contemplative mood, in the foreground with dull earthen jacket and mustard clothes enhances the message of the futility of worldly pleasures when compared to the life of a hermit immersed in the fondness of the Almighty.

The margins of both the paintings are richly decorated with geometrical and floral motifs, and have enhanced the richness of the painting.

INSCRIPTIONS ON THE PAINTINGS

Painting No. 7

Wa barge darakhtan khurde yake az paadshaahaan aan bataraf ba huqme
Ziyarat nazdike uu raft wa guft agar masalihat biinii bashahare dar ayee

One of the holy men of Syria had passed many years of devotion in the wilderness, and was feeding on the leaves of trees. The king of that country, in the way of a pilgrimage, visited him, and said, If you can see the propriety of removing into my capital. . . .[64]

Painting No. 8

Az hayaatey nakhustin begardiid wa surkh wa safed baraamad wa farab shud Wa bar baalishey diiba takiya zada wa ghulameyparii paikar wa marwahe taausey

. . . and found the hermit much altered from what he first saw of him. His face had become fair and ruddy, and his body plump and jolly; and he was reclining at his ease on cushions of brocade, and had the Hoori-like damsel lolling by his side, and the fairy-formed youth holding a fly-flap of peacock's feathers in his hand, and standing by him in attendance. . . .[65]

TRAVAILS OF A FORTUNE SEEKER

THE NINTH and tenth paintings illustrate story xxviii of chapter III, and have been translated by Ross as below:[66]

> They tell a story of an able-bodied youth[67] who had, from adverse fortune, fallen into great affliction, and from an inordinate appetite and a narrowness of means to satisfy it, had reason to complain. He stated his grievances to his father, and craved his permission, saying: I wish to travel, that peradventure I may, by the strength of my arm, lay hands upon the skirt of my object: "Science and knowledge are useless till put in practice. Aloes-wood they place upon the fire, and musk they rub, in order to extract their fragrance."[68]
>
> The father replied: O my son, put this absurd fancy out of your head, and draw the foot of contentment within the mantle of safety, for philosophers have said, Fortune is not to be secured by exertion, but its want is to be obviated by moderation:[69] "Nobody can seize on the skirt of fortune by force. Exertion is here as useless as putting antimony on a blind man's eyebrows [that it may give a lustre to the eyesight]. Were two hundred accomplishments appending to every hair of thy head, skill is of no practical use where bad luck prevails.[70] What can a powerful but unlucky man do? The hand of fortune is more effective than the arm of strength."[71]
>
> The son said: O father, the advantages of travelling are manifold: from the enjoyments of the mind, and allurements of kind acts; from beholding strange sights, and hearing wonderful adventures; from the

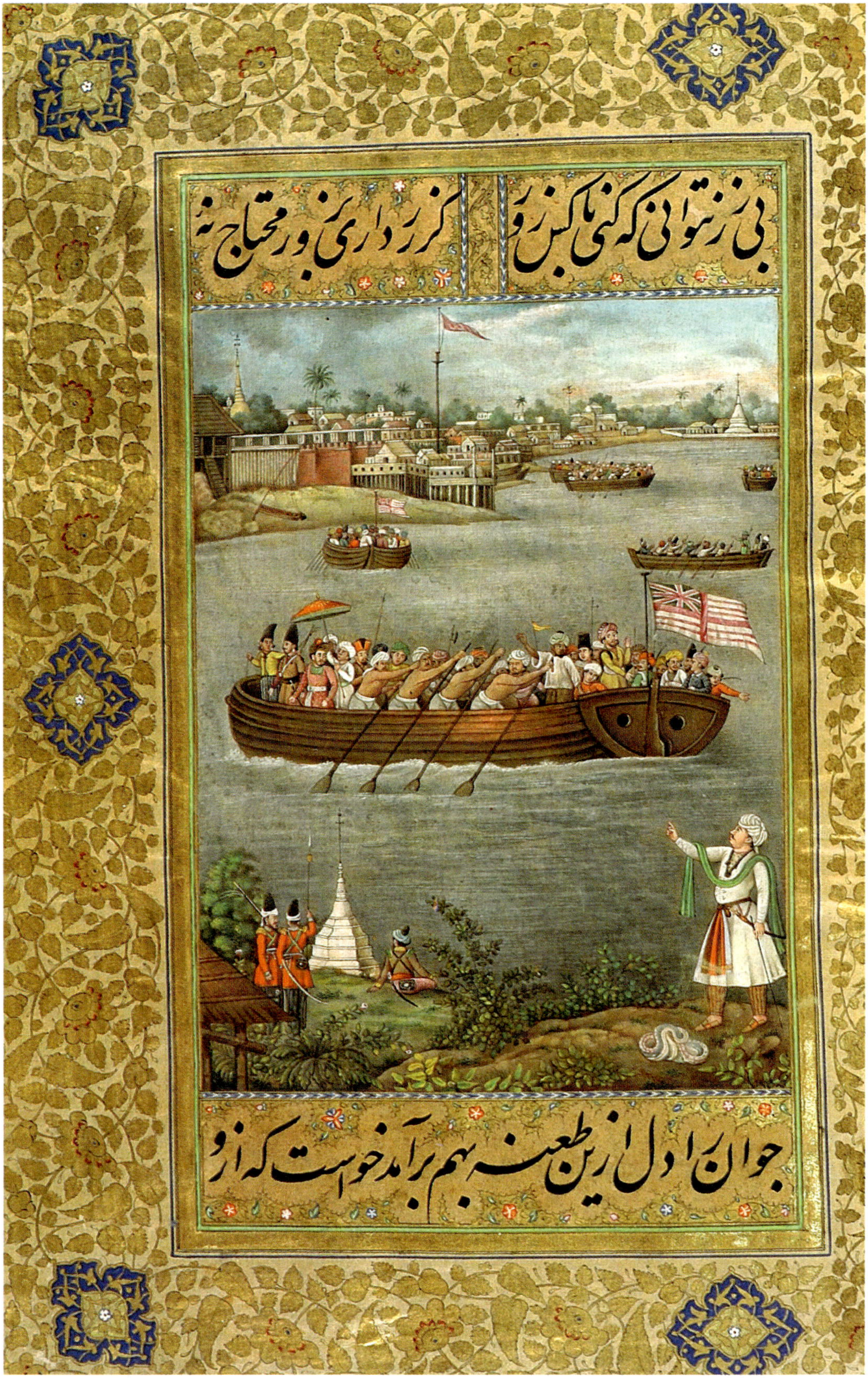
بی زر نتوانی که کنی ناکس رو
گر زر داری ور محتاج نه
جوان را دل ازین طعنه بهم برآمد خواست که از و

Painting 9

recreation of cities, and recognizance of former places; from the acquisition of dignity and urbanity, and the augmentation of wealth and property; and from a renovation of old acquaintance, and an experience of the times;[72] as our guides in the paths of righteousness have pointed out. "Whilst thou loiterest at home and in thy shop, like a pledge in pawn, never, O raw youth, canst thou arrive at man's estate: roam abroad in the world, and take thy fill of its enjoyments before the day shall come when thou must quit it for good."[73]

The father replied: O my son, such as you have stated them, the advantages of travelling are numerous: nevertheless, they are the special lot of five orders of mankind:[74] First, a merchant, who, in consequence of his wealth and property, has soul-alluring bondsmen and handmaids, and active menials about him in his service: and has every day a different city, and every night a change of stage, and at all times a place of recreation, where he can indulge in worldly luxury:[75] "Amidst mountains, wildernesses, or deserts, the rich man is no stranger: wherever he may go he can pitch himself a tent, and take up his abode; but he who has not at command the comforts and enjoyments of life, is alike unknown and an alien even at his own home."[76]

Secondly, the man of learning, who, in his mellifluous eloquence and attic wit, in his profound science and recondite knowledge, wherever he may go is generally sought for, and respected:[77] "The presence of a wise man is like pure gold, which is of the same price and value wherever it is found;[78] but the ignorant son of a nobleman is like paper or leather currency, which, in a strange place, will go for nothing."[79]

Thirdly, a handsome young man, whose society the hearts of the goods and holy will piously covet,[80] as they have said: A little beauty is preferable to much wealth; and they tell us, a lovely face is the solace of wounded hearts and the key of locked-up gates;[81] consequently, all will court its society, and esteem its service as a courtesy: "Wherever a lovely person shall roam he will meet honour and respect, notwithstanding his father and mother may have driven him in anger from his home. I found a peacock's feather within the leaves of a Koran, and said to it, This station is above thy condition. It replied: Be silent; for that person who possesses the charms of loveliness, wherever he puts his foot, finds no hand held up to oppose him."[82] "Where there is a fondness and partiality for the son, it costs us not a thought that the father is estranged from him;[83] he is a jewel, let him not make the world his casket, for everybody is the purchaser of such a nonpareil pearl."[84]

Fourthly, the charming songster, who, with the pipe of David and the fascination of his melody, can arrest the river in its current, and the bird in its flight; consequently, through the means of this perfection he can captivate the hearts of his admirers, and the lords of mystical knowledge will fondly court his society, and be assiduous in serving him.[85] "How grateful is the soft and plaintive voice, vibrating on the ears of lovers giddy from a morning debauch; a melodious pipe will fascinate more than a lovely face, for this can seduce the sensual appetite, but that must enrapture the soul."[86]

Fifthly, a common mechanic, who can earn a subsistence by the industry of his hand, and shall not have to stake his reputation for every morsel of bread,[87] as philosophers have said: "Though obliged to wander a stranger from his country, the cobbler or botcher would not suffer inconvenience or trouble; but were he, from anarchy, deposed from his throne, Mumruz the king[88] would perish of hunger."[89]

Such qualities, as I have detailed them, are, O my son, the solace of the heart, and the means of sweet enjoyment during a journey; but for any man that does not possess one of them to travel abroad were an idle undertaking, and none would ask his character, or inquire after him.[90] "That man whom the revolutions of the skies regard with a malignant aspect, fortune will conduct to anything but his good. The pigeon that is ordained never to revisit its nest, destiny is enticing towards the bait and snare."[91]

The son said: O father, why should I act in contradiction to the maxim of the wise, who have told us that though our lot be apportioned, yet there is a condition appending to it; and though misfortune be ordained, yet we are to turn aside from the door that leads to it:[92] "Though our daily bread will come to us without our thought, it is the duty of reason to look for its approaches; although none will die till their predestined time, there is no occasion to walk into the mouth of a dragon."[93] And circumstanced as I feel myself, I could assail a formidable elephant and grapple with a ferocious lion. Accordingly, it were advisable that I should travel, for I am not able to put up any longer with indigence.[94] "When a man falls in his rank and station, what can he apprehend that is worse? The world at large is his place of residence. The rich man at night repairs to his mansion; the poor man makes that place his inn where the night overtakes him. But what need has he of inn, resting-place, or abode? Wherever he may wander, all is the dwelling of his God."[95]

He so spoke, took leave of his father, asked his blessing, and departed. And as he went along they heard him that he was saying: "When fortune may not accord to his wish, the man of skill will travel where his name is not known."[96]

He was thus proceeding, till he reached a seashore, where rocks were heaved upon rocks by the force of its waves, and the roaring of its billows was heard for many furlongs:[97] "Such was the awfulness of the deep, that the water-flow found it not safe to rest on its bosom; and its smallest wave would roll millstones along its strand."[98]

Here he saw a number of people, each of whom had for a small piece of gold taken a passage in the ferry-boat, and had his luggage stowed by him.[99] The young man, having no money, opened the mouth of entreaty; but however much he supplicated them they showed him no favour, and said: "Without money thou canst not commit violence upon and force anybody; and if thou hast money, there is no occasion for force."[100] And the ungenerous master of the vessel turned towards him, as he pushed off his boat, and with a sneer, added:[101] "Thou hast no gold, and thou canst not cross the sea by main strength; what can the prowess of ten heroes avail thee? Bring me the passage money of one man."[102]

The youth was much hurt at this sarcasm of the boatman, and wished that he could revenge it; but the boat had put off. He called aloud, and said, If this garment which I am wearing will satisfy, I am ready to give it you. The boatman was avaricious, and brought his vessel back: [103] "Covetousness will sew up the eyes of the wary, and greediness decoy the bird and fish into the net."[104] So soon as the young man could lay hands on the boatman's beard and collar, he dragged him from his vessel and belaboured him most unmercifully: "Whenever thy hand can reach it, tear out thy foe's brain, for such opportunity washes anger from the mind." His comrade disembarked, that he might back him; but meeting the same rough treatment, he turned his back. They saw it advisable to make their peace with him, and compromise for his passage money: "When thou witnessest a dispute, show forbearance, for mildness will shut the door of contention; where thou seest a perseverance, oppose it with kindness, for a sharp sword cannot cut into a silk-quilted corselet.[105] Use a sweet tongue, courtesy, and gentleness, and thou mayst manage to guide an elephant with a hair."[106]

After excusing what had passed, they fell at his feet, and, after kissing with hypocrisy his head and face, they ushered him on board the boat, and proceeded on their voyage, till they came to the pillar, which rises in the sea out of some Grecian ruins. The boatman said: The vessel is here in some danger; it will be necessary for one of the heartiest, most heroic, and strongest of you to get upon this pillar and hold a hawser in his hand till we can swing her head round. The youth, in the pride of that courage which was uppermost in his thoughts, neither regarded the rancour of an injured rival, nor put in practice that maxim of the wise,[107] who have said, if you have given a person serious cause of offence, and should afterwards do him a hundred kind offices, rest not secure against his revenge of that one offence; for the dart may be extracted from the wound, yet the smart of it will rankle in the heart: "How well did the captain remark to his troop: When thou hast made a cut at thy antagonist, expect a thrust in return. Now that another is suffering pain at thy hand, trust not that thy heart shall be exempt from affliction. Throw not a stone upon the turret of the citadel, for a stone may perhaps be returned from the castle:"[108] So soon as the youth had put the hawser over his arm, and seated himself on the top of the pillar, the boatman dragged it from his hand and pushed off the vessel.

The deserted wretch stood aghast. For two days he suffered calamity and distress, and underwent much hardship. On the third day sleep overpowered and precipitated him into the sea.[109] After another day and night he reached the shore, when well-nigh reduced to his last gasp. Here he began to eat the leaves of trees and roots of grass, till, getting a little refreshed, he was able to set forward in the desert, and was proceeding when, overcome with hunger, thirst, and fatigue, he arrived at a well, where a crowd of people sat in a circle around it, and each had a draught of water presented to him in his turn, on paying a pashiz or small species of coin. The youth had no money; he begged a little water gratis, but this they refused; he attempted to reach it by force, but to no good purpose. Some few he of course knocked down, but they overpowered him with numbers, and beat him unmercifully, and maimed him sadly: "Notwithstanding his huge and formidable aspect, when gnats act in concert they will bring down an elephant; when ants set to work and move in a body, they can strip a fierce lion of his hide."[110]

Jaded and maimed, but impelled by necessity, he got up with the rear of a caravan, and made a shift to follow it.[111] In the evening they arrived at a place much infested with robbers. He beheld the people of the caravan with bodies trembling in fear, and minds occupied with their danger. He said: Be not alarmed, for I am one among you that can of myself encounter any fifty, and the other youths will assist me. The people were encouraged by his boasting, and, overjoyed with his company, they supplied him with foods and drink. The fire of the youth's stomach had blazed into a flame, and the rein of temperance dropped from his hand. He devoured many mouthfuls of the victuals, and gulped down several draughts of water, before he could appease the demon of his belly, when sleep seized him and laid him at rest.[112]

Belonging to that caravan there was an experienced old man, who had seen much of the world. He said: O my friends, I am more afraid of this your guard than of all the thieves beside, as they tell a story, that an

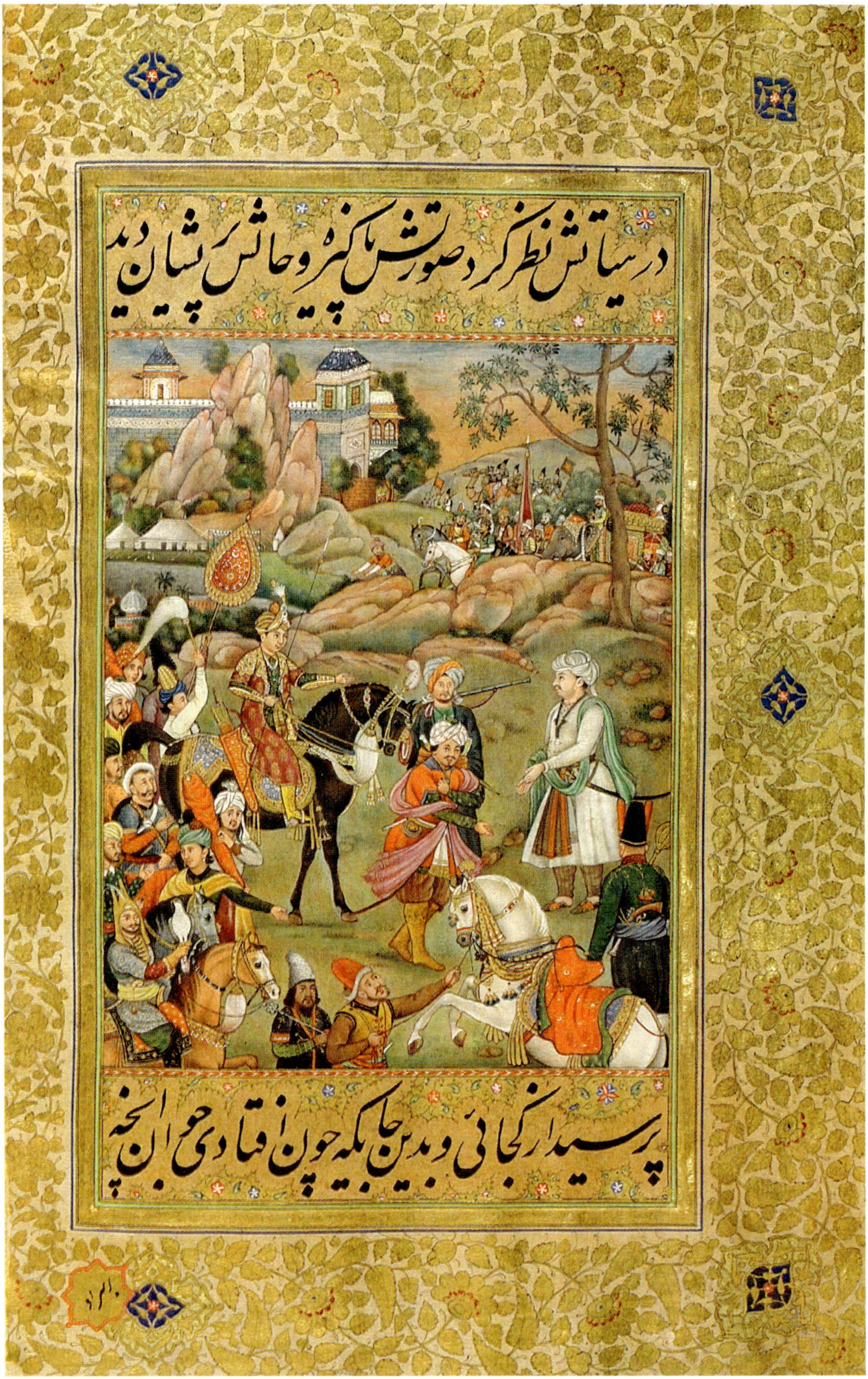

Painting 10

Arab had hoarded a sum of money, and could not sleep by himself at home from a dread of the Luriyans, a tribe of notorious robbers. He got one of his neighbours to abide with him, that in his society he might dispel the gloom of solitude. In this way they passed some nights together, till the friend found out where he kept his money, when he stole and made off with it. In the morning they found the Arab weeping and bewailing, and asked: How comes this? Perhaps the thief has made free with that money. He replied: Not he, by God! But my friend and guard has stolen it: "I can never sit down secure of my companion till I ascertain what may be his disposition. The bite of a foe's tooth must prove more cutting where it is given under the semblance of a friend."[113] Who can say but this may also be one of the thieves, who has introduced himself by a stratagem among us, that he may watch his opportunity of giving intelligence to his comrades. Accordingly, I see it advisable that we should leave him asleep and depart.

This counsel of the old man made a strong impression on his juvenile companions; and, as they stood in awe of his athletic power, they packed up their baggage and left the youth asleep. He did not get awake till the sun shone bright on his shoulders, when, raising his head, he found that the caravan was gone. In this forlorn state he wandered to some distance, and lost all trace of the path. Overcome with thirst and fatigue, he threw himself up for lost. He was saying: "Who will converse with me, now the camels are departed; the stranger has no friend, unless it be a stranger:[114] he will deal harshly by a stranger who has not been himself often a traveller and stranger."[115]

The desponding youth was uttering this speech while a king's son, who had dropped his retinue in the pursuit of hunting sport, was standing over him. He listened to these words, and, looking at his aspect, beheld a graceful figure, but a mind in much affliction. He asked him, saying: Whence are you, and how came you into this place? He made a short statement of the adventures, which had befallen him. The prince took compassion on him, gave him a dress and largess, and sent a confidential servant to take him home.[116]

His father was rejoiced at seeing him, and thanked god for his safe return. At night he entered in details of what befell him in the affair of the ferryboat, the insolence of the boatman, the violence of the peasants at the well, and treachery of the caravan people on the road. The father said: O my son, did not I warn you, at the time of your departure, that the courageous wrist of the empty-handed was manacled and his lion-like arm broken: "How happily did that empty-handed man of war remark, A barley-corn of gold is worth more than fifty man', or pounds', weight of strength."[117]

The son replied: O father! till you may somehow undergo trouble, you cannot acquire treasure; till you put your life in jeopardy you cannot subdue your enemy; and until you may sow the seed you cannot reap the harvest. Do you not perceive that, in return for the little fatigue I underwent, what a store of wealth I acquired; and for the sting I endured, what a stock of honey I secured:[118] "Though we cannot get more than our predestined portion, it behoves us not to be idle in looking after it. Were the diver to think on the jaws of the shark he would never lay hands on the precious pearl: the lower mill-stone takes not its turn in circulation, and sustains in consequence the brunt of the burthen: what would the ravenous lion have to eat if he remained a sluggard in the corner of his den, or what power of soaring after game has the broken-winged falcon? Wert thou to expect sport by staying at home thou wouldst become all legs and arms, like a spider!"[119]

The father said: O my son, on this occasion the skies co-operated, and fortune was your guide, so as to enable you to pluck a rose from your thorn and to extract the thorn from your foot. Moreover, an opulent gentleman met you and generously investigated your condition and redressed your broken fortune; otherwise, such instances are rare, and we ought not to expect and trust to wonders. Take heed that, led away by this greediness, you do not again enter the circle of desire, or spread the carpet of covetousness: "The sportsman does not every day make sure of his game. It may happen that the tyger shall one day tear him."[120]

In like manner as a certain king of Persia had a precious gem set in a ring. For the sake of recreation, he went on one occasion with a select

> retinue to the Mussala, near Shiraz, and ordered that they should fix the ring on the dome of Azud, with a proclamation that whoever might shoot an arrow through its hoop should have the ring as a present. It happened that four hundred professed archers who were in the royal train took their aim, but all of them missed it. A boy at play on the terrace roof of a public building was shooting from his bow at random, and lo! the morning breeze took his arrow and carried it through the circlet of the ring. They complimented him with the gem and ring, and made him many present. After this the boy burnt his bow and arrows. They asked: Why did you do so? He replied: That my first instance of reputation may be lasting. "It at one time may chance that the clear-headed sage shall be mistaken in the counsel he will offer; at another time we find that an unskilful boy shall, through mistake, hit the target with his arrow."[121]

The event has been painted in two parts. The ninth painting shows the banks of the water front where the youth is standing on the rocks and gesturing to the group to return back and give him a lift. There are a number of boats in the scene suggesting that the place is a regular port. Curiously enough, the flag this boat and the one a little ahead of it are flying resembles the Union Jack, the national flag of the British. The passengers on the boat other than the sailors and accompanying attendants are all affluent people who in the story have been shown to be doubtful towards any stranger and uncaring for those with little money.

In the foreground is the top of a temple with two soldiers standing in full dress and a third one sitting relaxed, suggesting that the area is a guarded outpost. In the far end, several large structures resembling forts, palaces and individual dwelling units have been shown, and the presence of a religious complex and *stupa*-like structures add to the completeness of an urban settlement. The youth, while requesting the boat to return after the brawl, had offered his rich garment as a price to the boatmen to carry him aboard. The painting shows his costly garment thrown on the ground in front of his feet as an offer to the boatmen if they heed to his request and return. The story later mentions that the boat approached some Grecian structures and the structures in the background show some closeness to Greek architecture. The artists, it appears, had studied the various forms or at least seen some of the contemporary port towns.

The tenth painting shows the scene of the outskirts of a town where the youth, abandoned and deserted, met the Prince. With hands folded and standing in gratitude for the courtesies extended to him by the Prince, the youth has a very expressive posture. The painting shows the Prince asking the youth about his nativity and wherewithal and a saddled white horse with an attendant ready for a rider, indicating the offering made by the Prince. A great deal of happenings has been packed in this single painting. The walls of the city in the background, rising rocks, green trees, scattered shrubs, a caravan in the background with a mounted elephant giving an impression of a royal group, and embedded with this background is the theme of the narrative – the Prince graciously bestowing the horse for a comfortable and safe journey and a patronizing glance on the youth standing courteously before the Prince.

INSCRIPTIONS ON THE PAINTINGS

Painting No. 9

> *Bezar natwaanii nakunii bakasey zor gar zardaari bazor mohtaaj na*
> *Jawan raa dil aziin taana baham bar aamad khaast key azuu*

> . . . however much he supplicated them they showed him no favour, and said: "Without money thou canst not commit violence upon and force anybody; and if thou hast money, there is no occasion for force." And the ungenerous master of the vessel turned towards him, as he pushed off his boat, and with a sneer, added: "Thou hast no gold, and thou canst not cross the sea by main strength; what can the prowess of ten heroes avail thee? Bring me the passage money of one man." The youth was much hurt at this sarcasm of the boatman, and wished that he could revenge it. . . .[122]

Painting No. 10

Dar siyatash nazar kard wa suurtash paakiz wa haalash pariishaan diid
Pursiid aza kujai wa badin jayakey chuun uftaadi jawan unach

. . . and, looking at his aspect, beheld a graceful figure, but a mind in much affliction. He asked him, saying: Whence are you, and how came you into this place?. . .[123]

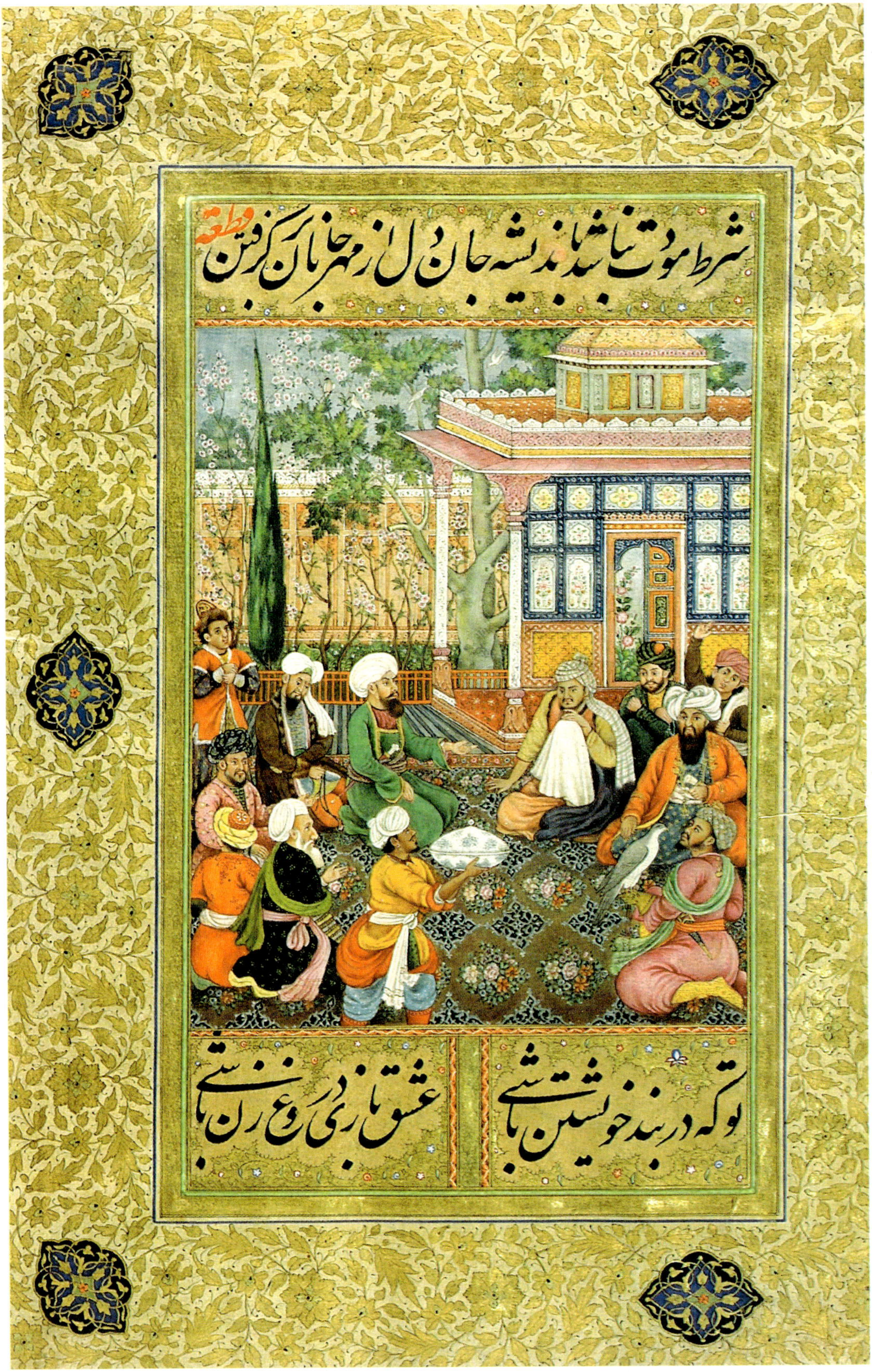
قطعه
شرط مودت نباشد باندیشه جان دل ز مهر جانان برگرفتن
تو که در بند خویشتن باشی
عشق بازی دروغ زن باشی

Painting 11

THE PANGS OF PASSION

ELEVENTH AND TWELFTH paintings are appended to the story iv of chapter V, "On Love and Youth". Ross's translation of the section reads as below:[124]

> A certain person had lost his heart and abandoned himself to despair. The object of his desire was not such a dainty that he could gratify his palate with it, or a bird that he could lure it into his net, but a frightful precipice and overwhelming whirlpool "When thy gold attracts not the charmer's eye, dust or gold is of equal value with thee."[125]
>
> His friends admonished him, saying: Put aside this vain fancy, for multitudes are in the durance and chains of this same passion, which you are cherishing.[126] He sighed aloud, and replied: "Say to my friends, Do not admonish me, for my eye is fixed on the wish of her. With strength of wrist and power of shoulders warriors overwhelm their antagonists and charmers their lovers."[127] Nor can it be consistent with the condition of love that nay thought of life should divert the heart from affection for its mistress "Thou, who art the slave of thine own precious self, playest false in the affairs of love. If thou canst not make good a passage to thy mistress, is the duty of a lover to perish in the attempt. I persist when policy is no longer left me, though the enemy may cover me all over with the wounds of swords and arrows. If I can reach her I will seize her sleeve, or at all events proceed and die at her threshold."[128]
>
> His kindred, whose business it was to watch over his concerns, and to pity his misfortunes, gave him advice, and put upon him restraints, but

> all to no goods purpose:[129] "The physician is, alas! Prescribing bitter aloes, and his depraved appetite is craving sweetmeats! Heardest thou what a charmer was saying in a whisper to one who had lost his heart to her: So long as thou mantainest thine own dignity, of what value can my dignity appear in thine eye?"
>
> They informed the princess[130] who was the object of his infatuation, saying: A youth of an amiable disposition and sweet flow of tongue is frequent in his attendance at the top of this plain; and we hear him delivering brilliant speeches and wonderful sallies of wit; it would seem that he has a mystery in his head and a flame in his heart, for he appears to be distractedly in love. The princess was aware that she had become the object of his attachment, and that this whirlwind of calamity was raised by himself, and spurred her horse toward him.[131] Now that the youth saw that it was the princess's intention to approach him, he wept, and said: "That personage who inflicted upon me a mortal wound again presented herself before me; perhaps she took compassion upon her own victim." However kindly she spoke, and asked saying: Who are you, and whence come you? What is your name, and what your calling? The youth was so entirely overwhelmed in the ocean of love and passion that he absolutely could not utter a word:[132] "Couldst thou in fact repeat the seven Saba, or whole Koran by heart, if distracted with love, thou wouldst forget thy alphabet."[133] The princess continued: Why do you not answer me? For I too am one of the sect of darweshes, may, I am their most devoted slave. On the strength of this sympathizing encouragement of his beloved, the youth raised his head amidst the buffeting waves of tempestuous passion, and answered. "It is strange that with thee present I should remain in existence; that after thou camest to tax, I should have speech left me."[134] This he said, and, uttering a loud groan, surrendered his soul up to God: "No wonder if he died by the door of his beloved's tent; the wonder was, if alive, how he could have brought his life back in safety."[135]

The eleventh painting shows the youth sitting on the floor in the company of his friends, both young and old, and in a dejected posture. The courtyard of the house gives an impression of prosperity and the sartorial adornments of the people present shows a mixed hierarchy, both in terms of the economic standards and in terms of age. The youth himself is carelessly dressed, befitting his mood.

A young lad standing on the left corner of the gathering and trying to assess the situation adds to the mystique of the state. By placing a person on the right foreground with a falcon resting on his wrist, the artist is conveying the possibility of a communication to the beloved. Another man bringing a covered dish with food in the left foreground gives an impression that the youth has been either frugal in his eating habits or has starved himself in the pain of his beloved. The concentration of every individual in the painting, whether looking at the youth or not, is towards the pitiable sufferings of love.

The carpet in the painting is rich and shows a harmonious selection of shades by the artist. Besides, the alignment of the cheerful and blooming flowers along the wall of the campus and around contrasts well with the expressions of the sad, introspecting youth. Men on the left are trying to counsel him and convince him to give up his impractical passion.

The twelfth painting, in continuation to the eleverth, shows the Princess riding on the horse, and accompanied by the bodyguards, in the market place, face to face with the youth. The background shows the main entrance, typical of contemporary architecture. The dynamic location adds to the meaning of the painting.

The costumes of the Princess reveal a great deal about the fashion of the period. The horse is standing in a state of readiness, while the Princess is holding the reins making the animal steady. A number of attendants are standing in the service of the Princess, holding the umbrella, waving the flywhisk for the comfort. The youth has fallen on the ground, speechless finding himself suddenly face to face with the love he has been longing for, and is either counting his last breaths or has just departed to his heavenly abode. The last words, "It is strange that with thee present I should remain in existence; that after thou camest to tax, I should have speech left me" speak through the present creation by the artist. The surrounding crowd is somewhat astonished with the happening. However, people in the far background are blissfully unaware of the happenings and are busy with their own tasks. The costumes and headgear imparts a cosmopolitan character to the gathering, and has traces of European influence.

The margins of the painting are richly decorated with the signature of the

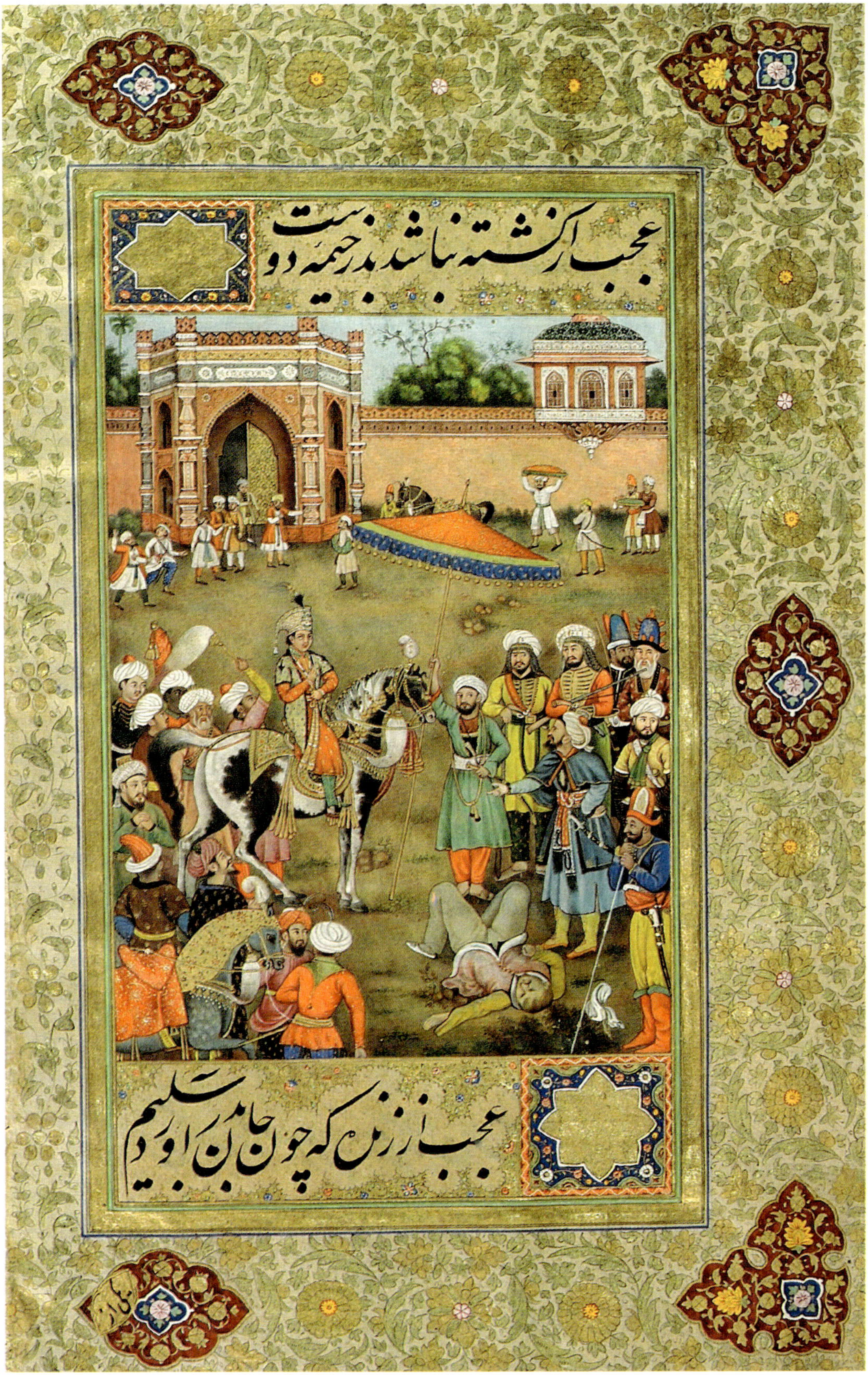
عجب از کشته نباشد بدر خیمه دوست
عجب از زنده که چون جان بدر آورد سلیم

Painting 12

main artist on the left hand fore corner. The floral patterns, though typical in the work, are yet unique and do not overpower the main painting. The light shades give a transparent impression and keep the primacy of the theme of the painting intact.

The profuse use of gold in this and almost all the other miniatures makes the contrast with red and blue used in the main paintings more visible. The shades of gold used are soothing to the eyes and are almost standard in all miniatures.

INSCRIPTIONS ON THE PAINTINGS

Painting No. 11

Shartey modat binaa shid ba andeshaye jaaney dil az meharey jaanaan bar giraftan
Tuu key dar band kheshtan baashi ishq baazi darogh zan baashi

. . .Nor can it be consistent with the condition of love that nay thought of life should divert the heart from affection for its mistress. "Thou, who art the slave of thine own precious self, playest false in the affairs of love. If thou canst not make good a passage to thy mistress, is the duty of a lover to perish in the attempt. . .

Painting No. 12

Ajab az kushta na bashad bey darey kheymaye dost
Ajab az zind key chun jaan aawarad saliim

. . . No wonder if he died by the door of his beloved's tent; the wonder was, if alive, how he could have brought his life back in safety. . . .

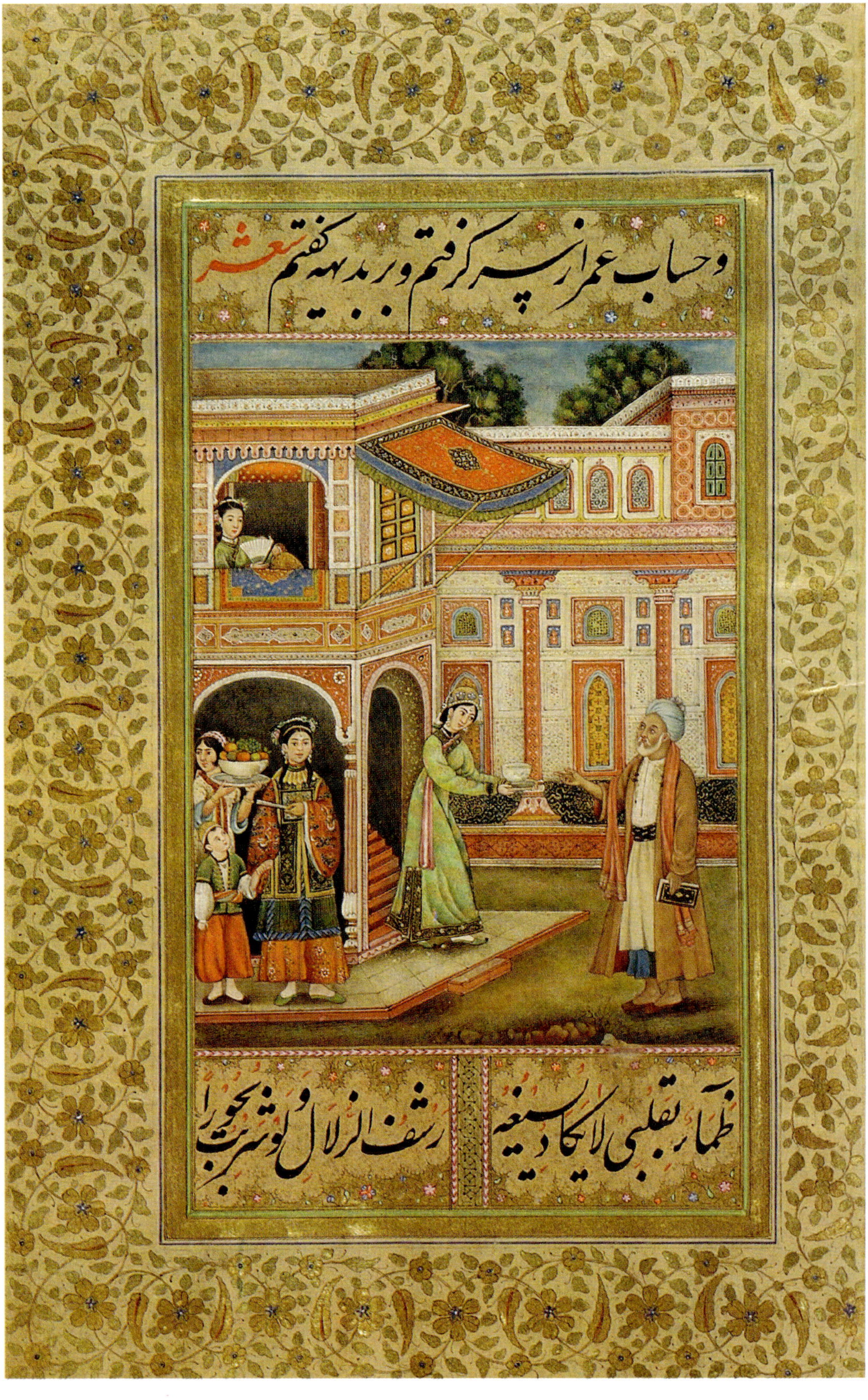

Painting 13

LOVE AND YOUTH

THE THIRTEENTH PAINTING depicts story xv of chapter V, entitled "On Love and Youth" and the narration reads as follows:[136]

> In my youth I recollect I was passing through a street, and caught a glimpse of a moon-like charmer during the dog-days, when their heat was drying up the moisture of the mouth, and the Samum, or desert hot-wind, melting the marrow of the bones.[137] From the weakness of human nature I was unable to withstand the darting rays of a noon-tide sun, and took refuge under the shadow of a wall, hopeful that somebody would relieve me from the oppressive heat of summer, and quench the fire of my thirst with a draught of water. All at once I beheld a luminary in the shadowed portico of a mansion, so splendid an object that the tongue of eloquence falls short in summing up its loveliness; such as the day dawning upon a dark night, or the fountain of immortality issuing from chaos.[138] She held in her hand a goblet of snow-cooled water, into which she dropt some sugar, and tempered it with spirit of wine; but I know not whether she scented it with attar, or sprinkled it with a few blossoms from her own rosy cheek. In short, I received the beverage from her idol-fair hand; and, having drunk it off, found myself restored to a new life. "Such is not my parching thirst that it is to be quenched with the limpid element of water, were I to swallow it in oceans.[139] Joy to that happy aspect whose eye can every morning contemplate such a countenance as thine. A person intoxicated with wine lies giddy and awake half the night; but if intoxicated with the cup-bearer [God], the Day of Judgment must be his dawn or morning."[140]

The painting shows the author passing through the alley of the charming beauty he has referred to nostalgically, and being offered a "goblet of snow-cooled water" by her. The book in the left hand is to reaffirm the elitist orientation of the author. The surrounding architecture is rich and shows that it is a locality of prosperous inhabitants. A close look at the dresses of the two ladies standing under the arch while the author and his cherished lady exchange courtesies, shows that one of them, holding the hand of a child, is either a friend or close relative, and the other holding the tray of fruits, is a maid.

Another lady sitting in the window on the first floor is holding a fan, typical of the Chinese or Japanese. The colourful red and green awning adds to the richness of the household.

INSCRIPTION ON THE PAINTING

Wa hisaabey umr aj sipar giraftam wa bar badih guftam
Zama bey qalbi laa yakaadi rashful zulaal walo sharbatey bijuraa?

. . . or the fountain of immortality issuing from chaos. She held in her hand a goblet of snow-cooled water, into which she dropt some sugar, and tempered it with spirit of wine; but I know not whether she scented it. . . .[141]

THE QAZI OF HAMADAN

FOURTEENTH AND FIFTEENTH paintings are appended to the story xix of chapter V, entitled "On Love and Youth" and the narration reads as follows:[142]

> They tell a story of the *cazy* of the city of Hamadan, that he was enamoured of a farrier's daughter, and had the horse-shoe of his heart made glowing hot in the fire of a forge. For a time he was wavering and unsettled, desiring and expectant, and repeating, as applicable to what was passing: "This straight and lofty cypress marched graceful before my eyes; she took the heart from my hand and trod it under her foot. This bold and lascivious eye was luring my heart into a snare. If thou wishest not to resign thy heart to anybody thou must shut thy eyes."[143]
>
> I have heard that she met the *cazy* on the highway. Something of this business had reached her ears, and she was beyond measure offended. She abused him vilely, spoke to him harshly, took up stones to throw at him, and showed him all manner of rudeness. The cazy observed to a respectable learned man who attended him on horseback: "Behold that charmer, how overwhelmed she is with anger; attend to that frown on her sour and sweet eyebrow:" as the Arabs say: the blow of our beloved has the relish of raisins: "to receive a slap on the mouth from thy hand is more sweet than to fill it with bread from my own:"[144] Thus does her outrageous violence give out the fragrance of courtesy; like kings who will denounce hostilities when they perhaps in their hearts are courting peace. "Unripe grapes have a tart taste; have patience for a few days, that they may become sweet."[145]

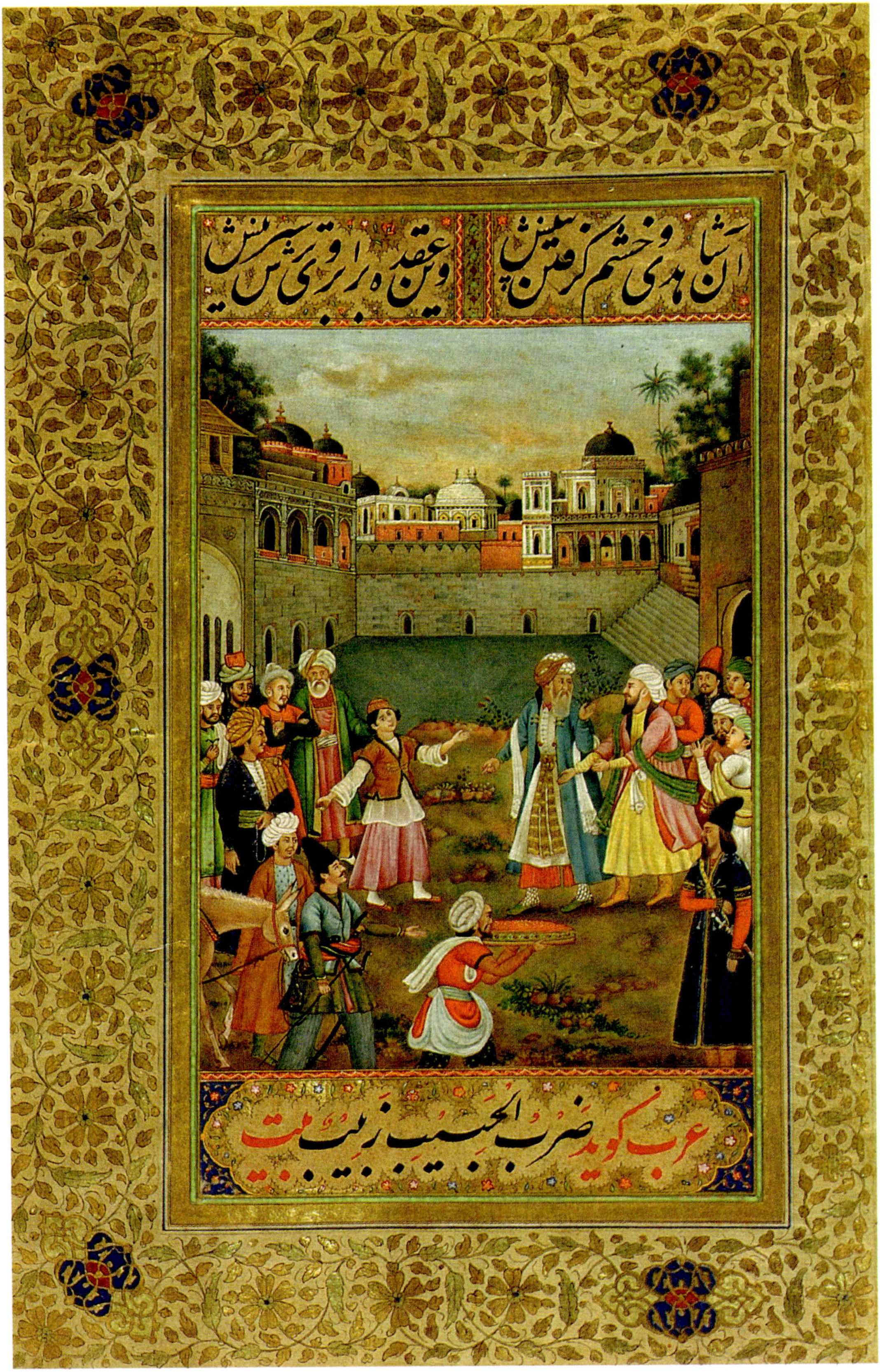

Painting 14

He thus delivered himself, and returned into the *cazy*'s court. Several well-disposed and respectable persons, who held offices under him, kissed the earth of obeisance, saying: With submission, and as in duty bound, we would make a representation to your lordship, that although "it might be deemed unpolite, as the sage have remarked: it is not proper to argue every point; to find fault with great men is itself a fault:"[146] yet, conscious that the past munificence of our lord and master was the cause of the good fortune of his servants, it were species of treachery in us to be aware of what is right, and not to notice it. And this is the path of rectitude, that you should shun the circle of delusion,[147] and fold up the carpet of criminal conversation with this damsel; for the station of a judge is of such high dignity that you should not contaminate it with an abominable sin. This object, which you have in contemplation, you should consider as your bane, and her story such as you have heard it:[148] "A person has committed many disreputable crimes; what regard has she for the reputation of another. Many is the good character of fifty years' standing which one shameless act will tread under foot."

The *cazy* approved of the unanimous advice of his friends, and commended their good sense and watchful fidelity, and said: The light in which my beloved friends view the policy of my situation is the mirror of what is right, and argument unanswerable[149]: "Of a truth, were friendship to be forfeited on our offering admonition, then might the righteous be accused of falsehood:" nevertheless, "admonish me as much as thou choosest, thou never canst wash a blackamoor white. I never can be made by anybody to forget thee; I am a snake with my head bruised, and cannot twist myself away."[150]

Having thus delivered himself, he deputed certain people to ascertain the damsel's circumstances, and was lavish of his cash, as has been remarked: Whoever has gold in the scales commands the arms of the balance; and he who cannot corrupt the world has not a friend all throughout the world:[151] "Whoever sees gold lowers his head, though, like the scales of Justice, he has iron-bound shoulders."

In short, he one evening accomplished a private interview; and that same night it was reported to the superintendent of the police that the *cazy* had all the evening had wine in his head, and his mistress in his arms; that he had lain awake in ecstasy, and was singing incessantly:[152] "Perhaps this cock does not to-night crow at his proper hour; the lover is not yet done with his dalliance. The temple of his mistress, lucidly fair within her curling ringlet, resembles the ivory-ball inlaid upon the ebony chowgong club. Be constantly on the watch, lest that lover of mischief fall into a doze, and the opportunity of enjoyment pass away in regret.[153] Till thou hearest the call for morning prayer at the metropolitan mosque, or the beat of the kettledrum over the palace-gate of the King Atabak, let lips be sealed to lips, like the eyelids of the salacious cock, and let them be removed only on the real crow of that silly bird!"[154]

Such was the state of the *cazy,* when one of his servants burst into his chamber, and called aloud: Why do you loiter in bed? Get up, and fly, now it is possible; for your rivals have calumniated you, nay, they have reported what is true.[155] Perhaps with the water of prudence we may quench the fire of mischief, which is yet low. God forbid that tomorrow, when risen into a flame, it should involve a whole world. The *cazy* turned towards him with a smile, and replied: "The lion has laid his paw on the game, what cares he for the yelping of a dog? Face to face enjoy thy mistress, and leave thy rival to gnaw the hand of jealousy."[156]

That same night they informed the king, saying: Such an act of wickedness has been perpetrated within your realm; what would your majesty order upon the occasion? The king answered: I know him to be one of the most learned of the time, and the non-pareil of his age. Possibly his rivals, from envy of his worth, have laid this plot, but till convinced by seeing it I cannot give ear to the fact: "Hastily to lay a hand on the sword of anger must lead to gnaw that hand with the teeth of regret."

I have heard that at break of day next morning, the king, accompanied with a select train, entered the *cazy's* bed-chamber. He saw that the tapers were alight, the charmer seated on the bad, the goblet broken, and the wine spilled, while the *cazy* lay stupefied in a dream of drunkenness, and altogether unconscious of the royal presence.[157] The king kindly waked him, and said: Get up, for the sun in risen. The *cazy* recollected how matters stood, and asked: From what quarter has he risen? The king was taken by surprise, and answered: From the east, as is usual! The *cazy* said: Praised be God! That the door of repentance is still open, according to the tradition: "The gate of repentance is not, nor shall it be, shut upon his [God's] servants, till the sun shall rise in the west: and he added: I ask pardon of God, and vow to him that I will repent: these two circumstances involved me in sin, my inauspicious fortune, and a weak understanding. If thou overtakest me with punishment, I am deserving of it; but if thou wilt forgive me, pardon is more desirable than chastisement."[158] The king replied: It is too late to repent, now that you know sentence of death is passed upon: The Most High has said: Then were it impossible their faith could avail, when they became witnesses of my commencing wrath: "How can it benefit the thief to repent at that time, when he cannot again throw his noose [by which he climbs up] into the balcony? Warn the tall man to withhold his hand from the fruit, for the dwarf cannot of himself reach the branch." When you fancied to yourself such a crime as has been proved, you could not have figured any path of escape.[159]

Having thus expressed himself, the king ordered the executioners of the law to lay hands on the *cazy.* He said: I have one plea more to submit to his majesty. The king asked: What may that be? He replied: "Notwithstanding thou spurnest me with the sleeve of thy displeasure, think not that I will quit the skirt of thy displeasure, think not that possible to fancy a deliverance from this sin that I am charged with, I can trust in that clemency which thou possessest."[160]

The king said: You have spoken with much genius, and an admirable flow of wit; yet is it repugnant to reason, and contrary to law, for me to permit eloquence and wisdom to rescue you this day from the hands of justice. I deem it wise to have you thrown headlong from the battlements of the citadel into the ditch, as an example for others. The *cazy* replied: O sovereign lord of the universe! I am the fostered child of this royal house, and have not been singular in the commission of this crime; let some person else be precipitated from the battlements, that I may take example by him.[161] The king smiled at this remark, and was pleased to signify his pardon; and he reproved his accusers, who expected his execution, and added: "All of you are laden with your

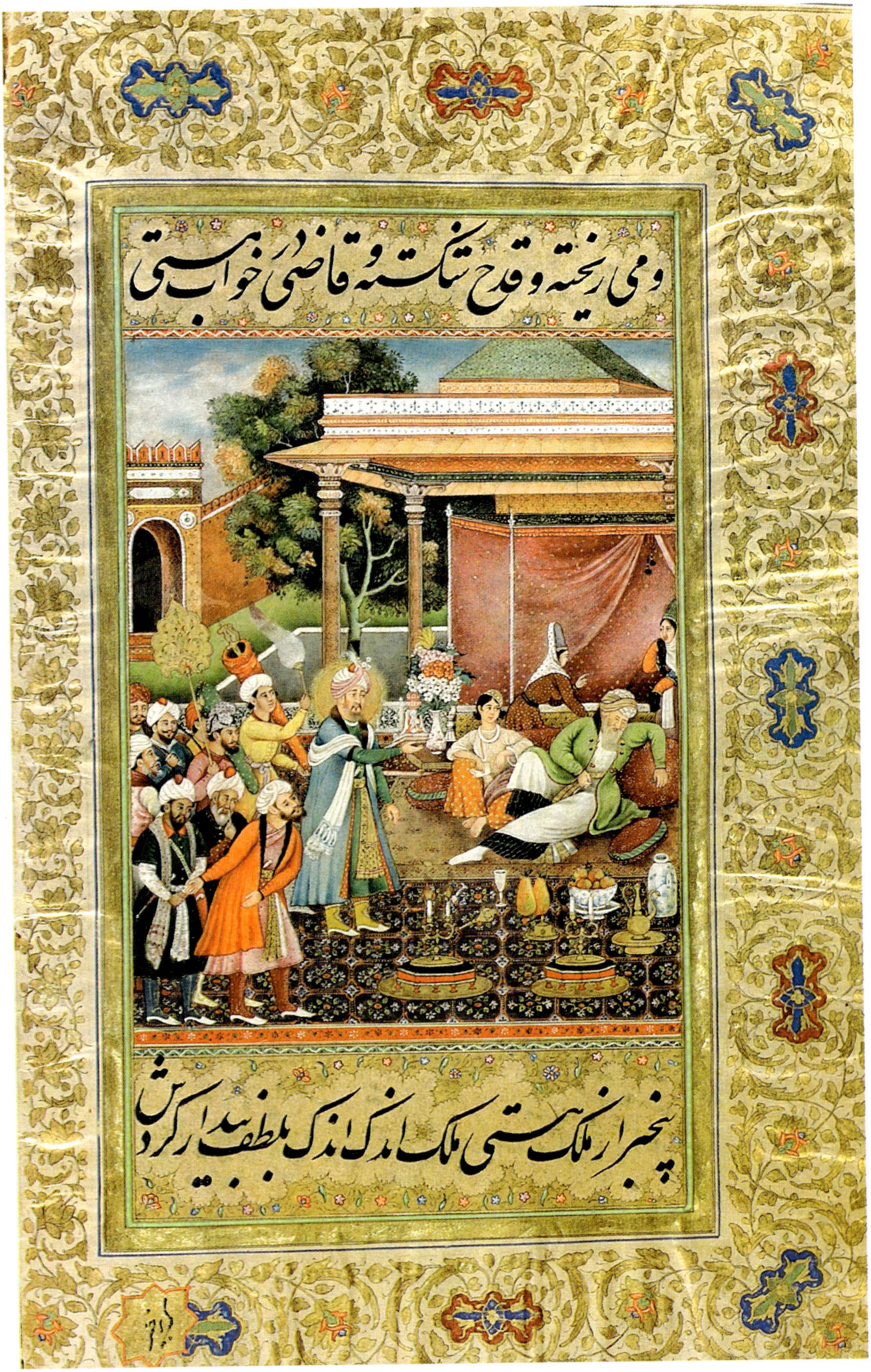

Painting 15

own sins; do not reproach others with their failings. Whoever is aware of his own failing will not find fault with the failings of other men."[162]

The fourteenth painting shows the environs of a public place next to the water reservoir, or *bawadi*, where infuriated by the provocative remarks of the *cazy*, the damsel is hurling stones at him, and the crowd is watching with both amusement and dismay. The friends and well wishers of the *cazy* are trying to dissuade him from entering into a further exchange with the damsel, and even perhaps requesting him to retreat. The passersby are looking with concern, as the office of the *cazy* is high and respectable.

The architecture of the water reservoir surrounded by the buildings, both residential and religious, is typical of the *bawadis* of Gujarat and Rajasthan region. The event is central to the painting and has been very proportionately conceived with the background. However, no extra elements have been introduced in the painting by the artist and thus, though the painting is rich in rendering, it gives a feeling of some gaps in the background.

The fifteenth painting shows the inebriated state of the *cazy*, drowned in the sensory pleasures, with the damsel, whom he had fallen for and had purchased for a price. The bed is lavish with cups, fruits and goblets of wine lying aside in abundance. The carpet is rich both in shades and in design. The floral decoration on the flower vases in the background has added to the romantic charm of the occasion.

The king with his retinue is staring at the *cazy* in admonition. The halo around the monarch is a typical style for ordaining upon him the highest stature close to divinity. The armed soldiers and bodyguards are in a state of alertness, and the attending maids are trying to hide from the king. The person in the foreground appears to be the friend or well wisher of the *cazy* warning him of the arrival of the king and the impending wrath of the monarch on his demeanour. Considering the disrepute the *cazy* had brought to the high office he held, some spectators in the group are looking down in shame. The posture and body language of the *cazy* suggest that he is not in control of his state and is helpless and yet prepared to mend with his faults. The king is in command of the situation, with an expression full of indignation. He is reprimanding the *cazy*, pronouncing the sentence, and dealing with the indiscipline firmly.

Painting No. 14

Aan shaahidey wa khasham giraftan biinash bin ukad bar abaruuye tursh shiriinasha
Arab goyad zarbul habib zabib

. . . how overwhelmed she is with anger; attend to that frown on her sour and sweet eyebrow:" as the Arabs say: the blow of our beloved has the relish of raisins. . . .

Painting No. 15

Wamaye rekhta wa qad shikast wa qazi dar khabey hasti
Bekhabar aj mulakey hasti malik andak beylutfe bedar gardish

. . . the goblet broken and the wine spilled, while the *cazy* lay stupefied in a dream of drunkenness, and altogether unconscious of the royal presence. The king kindly waked him. . . .

THE RICH AND THE POOR

SIXTEENTH PAINTING is a part of the discourse between Sa'adi and the darwesh about the qualities of the rich and the poor on their suitability to the path of righteousness, and forming the narration xxi of the chapter VII on "Of Impressions of Education." Ross has translated the discourse giving the qualities of rich in the following words:[163]

> I saw a certain person in the garb of darweshes, but not with their meekness, seated in a company, and full of his abuse. Having opened the volume of reproach, and begun to calumniate the rich, his discourse had reached this place, stating:[164] The hand of the poor man's ability is tied up, and the foot of the rich man's inclination crippled: "Men of liberality have no command of money, nor have the opulent and worldly-minded a spirit of liberality."[165]
>
> Owing, as I am, my support to the bounty of the great, I considered this animadversion as unmerited, and replied: O my friend! the rich are the treasury of the indigent, the granary of the hermit, the fane of the pilgrim, resting-place of the traveller, and the carriers of heavy burthens for the relief of their fellow-creatures.[166] They put forth their hand to eat when their servants and dependants are ready to partake with them; and the bounteous fragments of their tables they distribute among widows and the aged, their neighbours and kindred: "The rich have their consecrated foundations, charitable endowments and rites of hospitality; their alms, oblations, manumissions, peace-offerings, and sacrifices. How shalt thou rise to this pomp of fortune who canst perform only these two genuflexions, and them after manifold difficulties?"[167] Whether it respect their moral dignity or

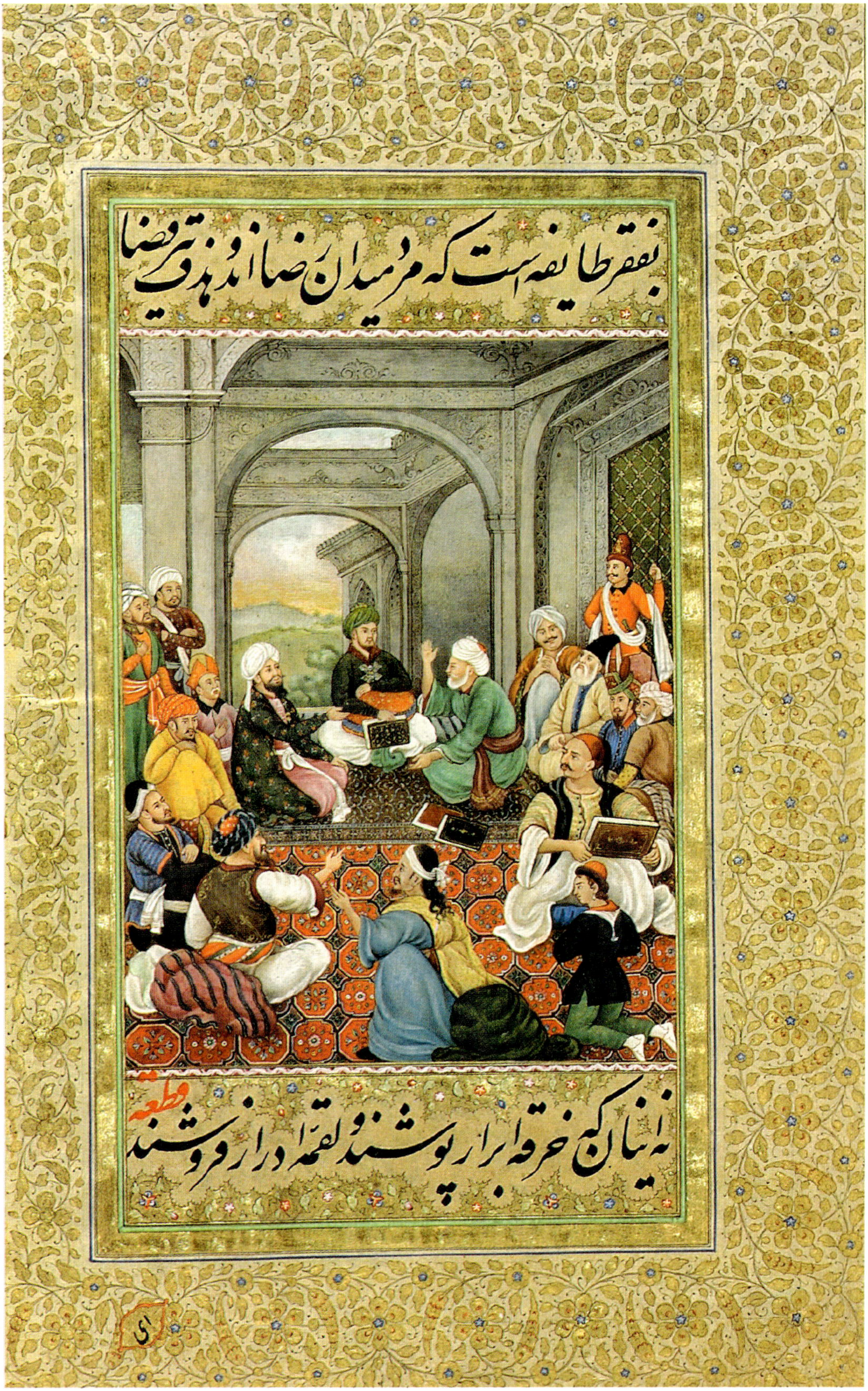

Painting 16

religious duty, the rich are at ease within themselves; for their property is sanctified by giving tithes, and their apparel hallowed by cleanliness, their reputations unblemished, and minds content.[168] The intelligent are aware that the zeal of devotion is warmed by goods fare, and the sincerity of piety rendered more serene in a nicety of vesture; for it is evident what ardour there can be in a hungry stomach; what generosity in squalid penury; what ability of travelling with a bare foot; and what alacrity at bestowing from an empty hand:[169] "Uneasy must be the night-slumbers of him whose provision for tomorrow is not forthcoming: the ant is laying by a store in summer that she may enjoy an abundance in winter."[170] It is clear that indigence and tranquillity can never go together, nor have fruition and want the same aspect: the one had composed himself for prayer, and the other sat anxious, and thinking on his supper; how then could this ever come in competition with that?[171] "The lord of plenty has his mind fixed on God; when a man's fortune is bankrupt, so is his heart:"[172] accordingly, the devotion of the rich is more acceptable at the temple of God, because their thoughts are present and collected, and their minds not absent and distracted; for they have laid up the conveniences of good living, and digested at their leisure their scriptural quotations [for prayer]. The Arabs say: God preserve us from overwhelming poverty; and from the company of him whom he loves not, namely, the infidel.[173] And there is a tradition of the prophet — that poverty has a gloomy aspect in this world and in the next![174]

My antagonist said: Have you not heard what the blessed prophet has declared? Poverty is my glory! I replied: Be silent, for the allusion of the Lord of both worlds applies to such as are heroes in the filed of resignation, and the devoted victims of their fate, and not to those who put on the garb of piety, that they may entitle themselves to the bread of charity. "O noisy drum! Thou art nothing but an empty sound; unprovided with the means, what canst thou affect on the last day of account? If thou art a man of spirit, turn thy face away from begging charity from thy fellow-creature; and keep not repeating thy rosary of a thousand beads."[175] Being without divine knowledge, a *darwesh,* or poor man, rests not till his poverty settles into infidelity;[176] for he that is poor is well-nigh being an infidel[177] – nor is it practicable, unless through the agency of wealth, to clothe the naked, and to liberate the prisoner from jail: how then can such mendicants as we are aspire to their dignity; or what comparison is there between the arm of the lofty and the hand of the abject?[178] Do you not perceive that the glorious and great God announces, in the holy book of the Koran, xxviii, the enjoyments of the blessed in Paradise? That to this community, namely, the orthodox Mussulmans, a provision is allotted;[179] in order that you may understand that such as are solely occupied in looking after their daily subsistence are excluded from this portion of the blessed; and that the property of present enjoyment is sanctioned under the seal of providence: "to the thirsty it will seem in their dreams as if the face of the earth were wholly a fountain".[180] You may everywhere observe that, instigated by his appetites, a person who has suffered hardship and tasted bitterness will engage in dangerous enterprises; and, indifferent to the consequences, and unawed by future punishments, he will not discriminate between what is lawful and what is forbid: [181] "Should a clod of earth be thrown at the head of a dog, he would jump up in joy, and take it for a bone; or were two people carrying a corpse on a bier, a greedy man would fancy it a tray of victuals."[182] Whereas the worldly opulent are regarded with the benevolent eye of Providence, and in their enjoyments of what is lawful are preserved from things illegal.[183] Having thus detailed my arguments and adduced my proofs, I rely on your justice for an equitable decree; whether you ever saw a felon with his arms pinioned; a bankrupt immured in a jail; the veil of innocency rent, or the arm mutilated for theft, unless in consequence of poverty: for lion-like heroes, instigated by want, have been caught under mining walls, and breaking into houses, and have got themselves suspended by the heels. It is moreover possible that a poor man, urged to it by an inordinate appetite, may feel desirous of gratifying his lust; and, unable to get himself a woman, he may fall the victim of some accursed sinia:[184] for the belly and privities are twin brothers, that is, pampered with good, these get rampant: as I have heard of a certain darwesh who was surprised in an act of abomination; in consequence of the shame that he was put to, and the dread of being stoned to death, he called aloud: O Mussulmans ! I have no money to buy myself a wife, nor sufficient forbearance to restrain my appetite; what can I do, for the monastic celibacy of Christians is not a rite of Islamism! And of the manifold means of mental tranquillity and corporeal enjoyment which are the special lots of the opulent, one is that every night they can command a fresh mistress, and every day possess a new charmer, such as must excite the envy of the glorious dawn, and stick the foot of the stately cypress in the mire of shame: "She had dipped her hands in the blood of her lovers, and tinged the tips of her fingers with jejubs:"[185] so that it were impossible, with such lovely objects before their eyes, for them to desire what is forbidden or to wish to commit sin: "Why should such a heart as the houries, or nymphs of Paradise, have captivated and plundered, show any way partial to the idols of Yaghma" [or a city in Turkistan famous for its beauties]?[186] "He who has in both his hands such dates as he can relish, will not think of throwing stones at the bunches of dates on their trees."[187] In common, such as are in indigent circumstances will contaminate the skirt of innocency with sin; and such as are suffering from hunger will steal bread:[188] "When a ravenous dog has found a piece of meat, he asks not, saying: Is this the flesh of the prophet Salah's camel or Antichrist's ass?"[189] Many are the chaste who, because of their poverty, have fallen into the sink of wickedness, and given their fair reputations to the blast of infamy:[190] "The virtue of temperance remains not with a state of being famished; and bankrupt circumstances will snatch the rein from the hand of abstemiousness."[191]

The moment I had finished this speech, the darwesh, my antagonist, let the rein of forbearance drop from the hand of moderation; unsheathed the sabre of his tongue; set the steed of eloquence at full speed over the plain of arrogance; and, galloping up to me, said:[192] You have so exaggerated in their praise, and amplified with such extravagance, that we might fancy them an antidote to the poison of poverty and a key to the store-house of Providence; yet they are a proud, self-conceited, fastidious, and overbearing set, insatiate after wealth and property, and ambitious of rank and dignity; who exchange not a word but to express insolence, or deign a look but to show contempt. Men of science they call beggars, and the indigent they reproach for their wretched raggedness. Proud of the property they possess, and vain of the rank they claim, they take the upper hand of all, and deem themselves everybody's superior. Nor do they ever condescend to return any person's salutation, unmindful of the maxim of the wise: That whoever is inferior to others in humility, and is their superior in opulence, though in appearance he be rich, yet in reality he is a beggar: "If a worthless fellow, because of his wealth, treats a learned man with insolence, reckon him the podex of an ass, although he be the ambergrise ox."[193]

I replied: Do not calumniate the rich, for they are the lords of munificence.[194] He said: You mistake them, for they are the slaves of dinars and dirams, or their gold and silver coins. For example, what profits it though they be the clouds of the spring, if they may not send us rain; or the fountain of the sun, and shine upon no one; or though they be mounted on the steed of capability, and advance not towards anybody? They will not move a step for the sake of God, nor bestow their charity without laying you under obligation and thanks. They hoard their money with solicitude, watch it while they live with sordid meanness, and leave it behind them with deadening regret, verifying the saying of the wise: That the money of the miser is coming out of the earth when he is himself going into it:[195] "One man hoards a treasure with pain and tribulation, another comes and spends it without tribulation or pain."[196]

I replied: You could have ascertained the parsimony of the wealthy only through the medium of your own beggary; otherwise to him who lays covetousness aside the generous man and miser seem all one.[197] The touchstone can prove which is pure gold, and the beggar can say which is the niggard. He said: I speak of them from experience; for they station dependants by their doors, and plant surly porters at their gates, to deny admittance to the worthy, and to lay violent hands upon the collars of the elect, and say: There is nobody at home; and verily they tell what is true: "When the master has not reason or judgment, understanding or discernment, the porter reported right of him, saying: There is nobody in the house."[198]

I replied: They are excusable, inasmuch as they are worried out of their lives by importunate memorialists, and jaded to their hearts by indigent solicitors; and it might be reasonably doubted whether it would satisfy the eye of the covetous if the sands of the desert could be turned into pearls: "The eye of the greedy is not to be filled with worldly riches, any more than a well can be replenished from the dew of night."[199] And had Hatim Tayi, who dwelt in the desert, come to live in a city, he would have been overwhelmed with the importunities of mendicants, and they would have torn the clothes from his back: "Look not towards me, lest thou should draw the eyes of others, for at the mendicant's hand no good can be expected."

He said: I pity their condition. I replied: Not so; but you envy them their property.[200] We were thus warm in argument, and both of us close engaged.[201] Whatever chess pawn he might advance I would set one in opposition to it; and whenever he put my king in check, I would relieve him with my queen; till he had exhausted all the coin in the purse of his resolution, and expended all the arrows of the quiver of his argument. "Take heed and retreat not from the orator's attack, for nothing is left him but metaphor and hyperbole.[202] Wield thy polemics and law citations, for the wordy rhetorician makes a show of arms over his gate, but has not a soldier within his fort:"[203] At length, having no syllogism left, I made him crouch in mental submission. He stretched forth the arm of violence, and began with vain abuse. As is the case with the ignorant, when beaten by their antagonist in fair argument, they shake the chain of rancour;[204] like Azor, the idol-maker, when he could not longer contend with his son Abraham in words he fell upon him with blows, as God has said in the Koran: If thou wilt not yield this point, I will overwhelm thee with stones: He gave me abuse, and I retorted upon him with asperity; he tore my collar, and I plucked his beard: "He had fallen upon me and I upon him, and a crowd had gathered round us enjoying the sport. A whole world gnawed the finger of astonishment when it head and understood what had taken place between us."[205]

In short, we referred our dispute to the *cazy*, and agreed to abide by his equitable decree: That the judge of the Mussulmans, or faithful, might bring about a peace, and discriminate for us between the poor and rich. After having noted our physiognomies, and listened to our statements, the *cazy* rested his chin on the breast of deliberation; and, after due consideration, raised it, and said: Be it known to you, who were lavish in your praise of the rich, and spoke disparagingly of the poor, that there is no rose without its thorn; intoxication from wine is followed by a qualm; hidden treasure has its guardian dragon; where the imperial pearl is found, there swims the man-devouring shark; the honey of worldly enjoyment has the sting of death in its rear; and between us and the felicity of paradise stands a frightful demon, namely, Satan.[206] "So long as the charmer slew not her admirer, what could the rival's malice avail him? The rose and thorn, the treasure and dragon, joy and sorrow, all mingle into one."[207] Do you not observe that in the garden there are the sweet-scented willows and the withered trunks; so among the classes of the rich some are grateful and some thankless; and among the orders of the poor some are resigned and some impatient:[208] "Were every drop of dew to turn into a pearl, in the market pearls would be as common as shells."[209] Nearby the throne of a great and glorious Judge are the rich meek in spirit, and the poor rich in resolution.[210] And the chief of the opulent is he who sympathises with the sorrows of the indigent; and the most virtuous of the indigent is he who covets not the society of the opulent: God is all-sufficient for him who trusts in God.

Then the *cazy* turned the face of animadversion from me towards the darwesh, and said: O you who have charged the rich with being active in sin, and intoxicated with things forbidden, verily there is such a tribe as you have described them, illiberal in their bigotry, and stingy of God's bounty; who are collecting and hoarding money, but will neither use nor bestow it. If, for example, there was a drought, or if the whole earth was deluged with a flood, confident of their own abundance, they would not inquire after the poor man's distress, and, fearless of the divine wrath, exclaim: "If, in his want of everything, another person be annihilated, I have plenty; and what does a goose care for a deluge? [211] Such as are lolling in their litters, and indulging in the easy pace of a female camel, feel not for the foot-traveller perishing amidst overwhelming sands:[212] The mean-spirited, when they could escape with their own rugs, would cry: What care we should the whole world die."[213]

Such as you have stated them, there is a tribe of rich men; but there is another class, who, having spread the table of abundance, and made a public declaration of their munificence, and smoothed the brow of their humility, are solicitous of a reputation and forgiveness, and desirous of enjoying this world and the next;[214] like unto the servants of his majesty the sovereign of the universe, just, confirmed, victorious, lord paramount and conqueror of nations, defender of the stronghold of Islamism, successor of Solomon, most equitable of contemporary kings, Mozuffar-ud-din Atabak-Abubakr-Saad, may God give him a long life, and grant victory to his standards! "A father could never show such benevolence to his son as thy liberal hand has bestowed upon the race of Adam. The Deity was desirous of conferring a kindness upon man, and in his special mercy made thee sovereign of the world."[215]

> Now that the *cazy* had carried his harangue to this extreme, and had galloped the steed of metaphor beyond our expectation, we of necessity acquiesced in the absolute decree of being satisfied, and apologised for what had passed between us; and after altercation we returned into the path of reconciliation,[216] laid the heads of reparation at each other's feet, mutually kissed and embraced, and, letting mischief fall asleep, and war lull itself into peace, concluded the whole in these two verses: "O poor man! Complain not of the revolutions of fortune, for gloomy might be thy lot wert thou to die in such sentiments. And now, O rich man! That thy hand and heart administer to thy pleasures, spend and give away that thou mayst enjoy this world and the next."[217]

The painting shows the author sitting in the company of the learned and engaged in the involved and intense discussion on the qualities and attributes of the rich and poor. Many of those participating in the debate are holding the books in their hand showing their literate status. In fact, two of the participants are holding the books as if it is some relevant treatise on the subject which they are consulting and quoting in their defense.

The precincts are presumably a public hall, or perhaps a part of a caravanserai, where the author had the chance of encountering the group of darweshes who were opposed to the rich and favored the poor. Significantly, all present are participating in the event, though the body language of the author is more forceful and dominating.

INSCRIPTION ON THE PAINTING

Bafaqrey taaipha ast ki mardey maidan razaa and wa hadaf tiirey qaza
Na inaan key khirak abraar poshand luqmaye idraar faroshand

> . . . but there is another class, who, having spread the table of abundance, and made a public declaration of their munificence, and smoothed the brow of their humility, are solicitous of a reputation and forgiveness. . . .[218]

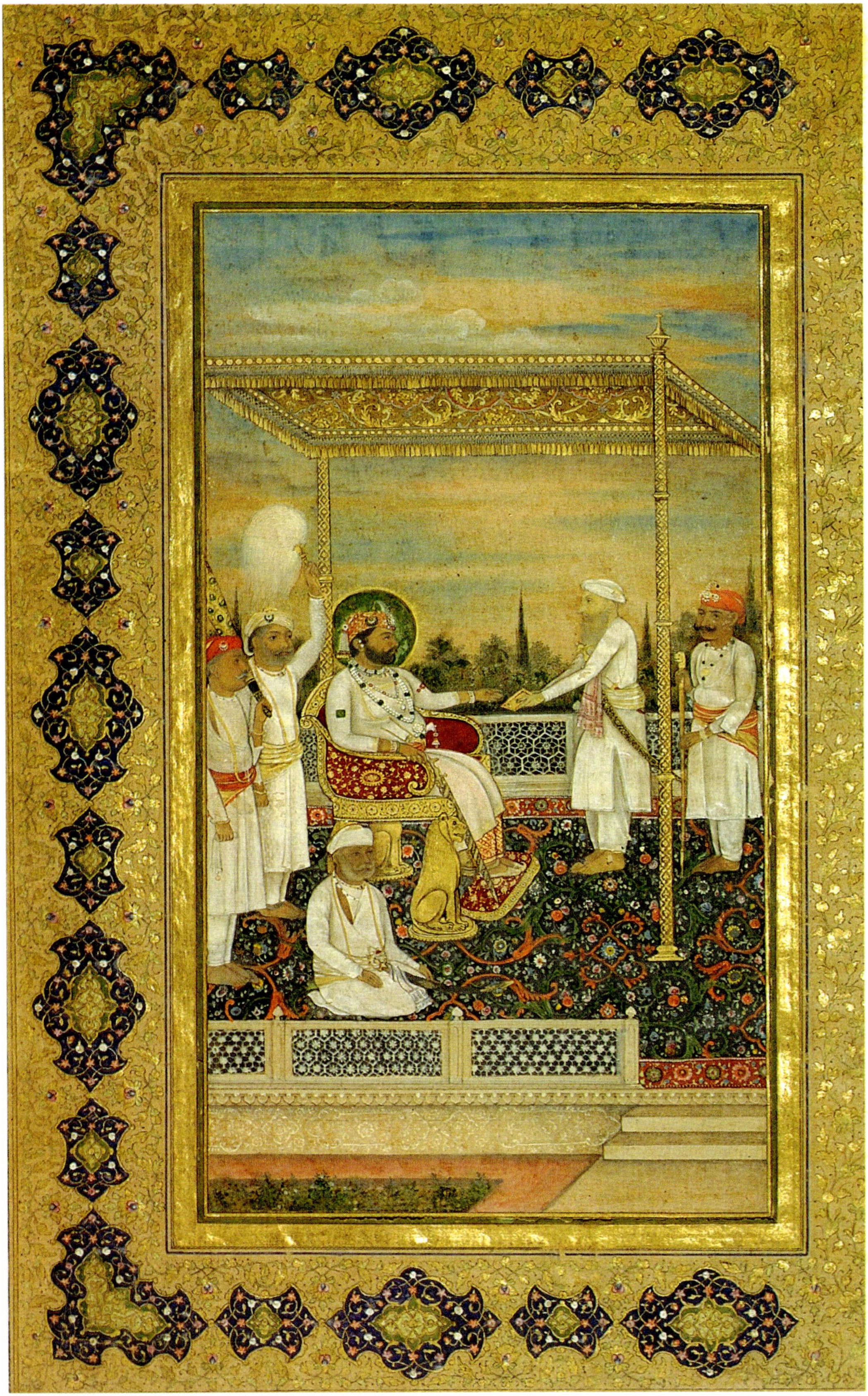

Painting 17

PRESENTING THE ILLUSTRATED MANUSCRIPT TO BANNI SINGH

THE SEVENTEENTH PAINTING shows the illustrator presenting the copy of the completed work of *Gulistan* to the ruler of Alwar, Banni Singh. There is no inscription on the painting, and some of the features of the Mughal School are discernible in the work.

The royal chair made of precious metal and brocade, purported to resemble the throne, is due to European influence, a single-seater with backrest of the medium size. The canopy is rich and made of gold. The supporting pillars are also made of gold showing the lavish lifestyle of the patron of this piece of art.

The painter is wearing a humble white dress in typical Rajput and Mughal style. His headgear is also sober and befitting the occasion. The carpet is rich and exquisite in design. The margins of the painting are embellished with fine designs and profusely enriched by a golden colour.

The Chief Minister or Musahib of the Maharaja, Raja Bahadur Padma Singh is shown seated on the ground. The Darogah Deoriji Lachhman Todamal Baniya, as the head of the porters, is shown introducing the copyist to the Maharaja. Also identified in the illustration are chairi-bardar Ladoo Khawas, who is waving the *chamar* or the flywhisk. Standing next to him with the whisk of peacock feathers known as the *morchal*, a symbol of rank is Bal Govind Khawas.

The attendants are standing at a desirable distance and yet in a state of alertness. The Chief Minister squatting in the foreground is adding completeness to the small gathering on the occasion showing that the presentation is a personal affair rather than a public celebration.

The filigree work on the railings around the platform where the king is sitting for the occasion is a culmination of the rich art of fine marble inlay work that had become easily accessible to many small rulers other than the Mughal Emperors by this period.

The legs of the throne form a curious study. The figure of lion imparted to the chair is both artistic and ostentatious. It is artistic from the point of view of the painter who has maintained the figurative proportions of the animal. It is also a remarkable creation from the point of view of the craftsman who conceived the design of the chair-cum-throne, as most of the rulers of the Rajputana region exhibited their prowess by incorporating the element of the lion in some form or the other in their insignia and emblems.

The halo around the king is blue rather than golden as has been the case in the other paintings of the collection, perhaps with a view to differentiate the patron from the kings and monarchs of the bygone era.

NOTES

1 Edward B. Eastwick, *The Rose Garden of Sheekh Muslih'ud-din Sadi of Shiraz,* The Octagon Press, London, 1979, p. 8.

2 "Be the five days at least thy own" connoting an indefinite short period of time. Edward B. Eastwick, ibid., p. 8.

3 Sa'adi has used the phrase kajawah literally meaning the slings on each side of a camel, to carry a traveller, but here it would mean a fellow traveller. Cf. Francis Gladwin, "Intimate and familiar Partner of my Travels," *The Gulistan or Rose Garden.*, p. xiii.

4 Phrase has been translated as closet-companion. Edward B. Eastwick, op. cit., p. 8.

5 "Now that thou hast the faculty of speech, converse, O brother! with cheerfulness and joy, for tomorrow that the messenger of death shall present himself thou must of necessity restrain thy tongue", James Ross, *Sadi: Gulistan or Flower Garden,* Walter Scott, London, n.d., p. 69.

6 James Ross, op. cit., p. 69.

7 Edward B. Eastwick, op. cit., p. 11.

8 James Ross, op. cit., p. 69. Compare with the translation in Hadi Hasan, *The Golden Treasury of Persian Poetry,* p. 92:
Though silence is the merit in the eyes of the wise, when expedient 'tis best to speak.
Two things are contrary to reason: not to speak when to speak; to speak when not to speak.

9 Francis Gladwin, *The Gulistan or Rose Garden by Musle-huddeen Shaik Sady of Sheeraz,* Lok Virsa Publishing House, Islamabad, 2nd edn., 1988, p. xiv.

10 For the evolution and placement of the garden in the Mughal buildings, see, Neeru Misra and Tanay Misra, *The Garden Tomb of Humayun: An Abode in Paradise,* Aryan Books International, Delhi, 2003.

11 "It being the season of spring, when the asperity of winter had mitigated, and the time of roses rich display had arrived." Edward B. Eastwick, op. cit., p. 12.

12 *A garden where the murmuring rill was heard;*
While from the trees sang each melodious bird;
The whispering breeze beneath the branches shade
Of bending flowers a motley carpet made.
Edward B. Eastwick, op. cit., p. 13.

13 James Ross, op. cit., p. 71.

14 "As soon as I had promised these words, he cast the flowers from his lap, and took hold of the skirt of my garment, saying, 'when the generous promise, they perform.' " Edward B. Eastwick, op. cit., p. 14.

15 Ross in his translation has assumed that The same day two chapters, namely "The Accomplishments of Education" and "The Rules of Conversation were composed". James Ross, op. cit., p. 71.

16 James Ross, op. cit., p. 72.

17 The Prime Minister of Noushirwan, the King of Persia, and a contemporary of Muhammad.

18 Edward B. Eastwick, op. cit., p. 17.

19 James Ross, op. cit., pp. 73-4.

20 Edward B. Eastwick, op. cit., p. 17.

21 Francis Gladwin, op. cit., p. xix.

22 For a discussion on the relative seating in the court of the Mughals, see, Kavita Singh.

23 Jahangir and Shahjahan have been invariably portrayed with a halo behind their head, and the tradition soon became a standard for the portrayal of every head of the kingdom.

24 "Pay for the salt you take, in order that it may not become a custom, and the village be ruined." They said, "What harm will this little quantity do?" He replied, "The origin of injustice in the world was at the first small, and every one that came added to it, until it reached this magnitude," Edward B. Eastwick, op. cit., p. 52.

25 James Ross, op. cit., pp. 104-5. Eastwick's translation has an extra couplet appended to the story:
Not always will the wicked tyrant live;
The curse upon him will aye for survive.
Edward B. Eastwick, op. cit., p. 52. Compare with Gladwin, "The iniquitous tyrant remaineth not, but the curses of mankind rest on him for-ever." Francis Gladwin, op. cit., p. 38. Same translation has been rendered by Anderson. See, Major R.P. Anderson, *The Gulistan of Shaikh Sa'di: A Complete Analysis of the Entire Persian Text,* Iran-Pakistan Institute of Persian Studies, Islamabad, 1985, p. 84.

26 Cf. Gladwin: "when the monarch ordered him to pay the price of the salt, that the exaction might not become a custom and the village be desolated," Francis Gladwin, op. cit., p. 37.

27 Cf. Anderson: "Oppression was brought into this world from small beginnings, which every newcomer has increased. . . ." Major R.P. Anderson, op. cit., p. 84.

28 James Ross, op. cit., pp. 113-15.

29 Cf. Francis Gladwin, ". . . he taught him three hundred and fifty-nine sleights, reserving however one sleight for himself," op. cit., p. 49.

30 Cf. Edward B. Eastwick, "... had his adversary been a mountain of iron, would have uptorn it from the base," op. cit., p. 62.

31 Cf. Francis Gladwin, "The King commanded that a dress and a reward in money should be bestowed on the master; and reproved and derided the youth, for having presumed to put himself in competition with his benefactor, and for having failed in the attempt," op. cit., p. 50.

32 *On earth there is no gratitude, I trow;*
Or none, perhaps, to use it now pretend.
None learn of me the science of the bow,
Who make me not the target in the end.
Edward B. Eastwick, op. cit., p. 62.

33 Cf. Francis Gladwin, "The master being sensible that the youth was his superior in strength, attacked with the sleight which he had kept to himself," op. cit., p. 50. Edward B. Eastwick, "The master perceived that the young man was his superior in strength. He fastened on him with that curious grip which he had kept concealed from him," op. cit., p. 62. R.P. Anderson, ". . . grappled him with the rare sleight he had kept secret from him," op. cit., p. 109.

34 Cf. Francis Gladwin, "The youth not being able to repel it, the master with both hands lifted him from the ground, and raising him over his head, flung him on the earth," op. cit., p. 50. The same translation has been rendered by R.P. Anderson, op. cit., p. 109. Edward B. Eastwick, however, has translated as: "The youth knew not how to foil it. The preceptor lifted him with both the hands from the ground, this and raised him above his head, and dashed him on the ground," op. cit., p. 62.

35 James Ross, op. cit., pp. 128-30.

36 *What though I am borne not in the camel throng*
Yet I will strive to bear your loads along.
Edward B. Eastwick, op. cit., p. 77. Francis Gladwin has translated this as: "Although I am not mounted on a beast, I would endeavour to carry your burthens," op. cit., p. 70. R.P. Anderson has also given the same translation, op. cit., p. 144.

37 *Rags are the external signs of holiness*
Sufficient — for men judge by outward dress.
Strive to do well, and what thou pleasest, wear;
Thy head a crown, thine arm a flag might bear.

Virtue lies not in sackcloth coarse and sad;
Be purely pious and in satin clad:
True holiness consists in quitting vice;
The world and lust, not dress; let this suffice.
Let valiant men their breasts with iron plate:
Weapons of war ill suit the effeminate.

Edward B. Eastwick, op. cit., p. 78.

Francis Gladwin has rendered this as: "The outside of religion is a Durwaish's dress, this is sufficient with a mortal face: let your actions be good, and put on any dress you choose; either wear a crown on your head, or carry a flag on your shoulders; for it is not coarse clothing that constitutes the Zahid; be truly pious and dress in satin. Sanctity consists in forsaking the world, with its lusts and appetites, not merely in changing the dress. In warfare manhood is required; of what use would armour be to an hermaphrodite?", op. cit., p. 71. Cf. R.P. Anderson, "How knows a man what a garment contains? As much to say what knows a man of the state of another's heart or morals? The body (which contains a mortal's heart) here is elegantly compared to a garment," op. cit., p. 146.

38 Cf. Edward B. Eastwick, "In short, one day, we had journeyed till dusk, and slept for the night under a castle's walls. The graceless thief took up the water-pot of one of his comrades, saying that he was going for a necessary purpose, and went, in truth, to plunder," op. cit., p. 78. Francis Gladwin has rendered almost similar translation, op. cit., p. 71. R.P. Anderson adds: ". . . carried off the water pot of one of his companions, and then went in quest of plunder," op. cit., p. 146.

39 *He'd fain with tattered garment for a darwesh pass,*
And make the Kabah's pall the housings of an ass.

Edward B. Eastwick, op. cit., p. 78. Francis Gladwin has translated as follows: "Behold this person, who covered his body with a religious dress, made the veil of the Kaba a housing for the ass," op. cit., p. 71. R.P. Anderson has given the same translation, op. cit., p. 148.

40 *When one member of a tribe has done*
A foolish act, all bear like disgrace,
Seest thou how in the mead of one ox alone
Will lead astray the whole herd of a place?

Edward B. Eastwick, op. cit., p. 78. Francis Gladwin is more lucid "When one of any tribe commits an act of folly, there is no distinction between high and low, the whole being dishonoured. Have you not observed that a single ox belonging to a herd will contaminate all the oxen of the village?", op. cit., p. 72. R.P. Anderson has given a similar translation, op. cit., p. 148.

41 *Be there but one rough person in their train,*
For his misdeeds the wise will suffer pain,

Should you a cistern with rosewater fill,
A dog dropped in it would defile it still.
Edward B. Eastwick, op. cit., p. 79; and Francis Gladwin, "By the means of one disorderly person in the company, the hearts of many wise men become afflicted. If you fill a cistern with rose water, and a dog should fall into it, it would thereby become impure," op. cit., p. 72. R.P. Anderson has given a similar translation, op. cit., p. 148.

42 James Ross, op. cit., pp. 152-5.

43 ". . . had for years worshipped in the desert, and sustained life by feeding on the leaves of the trees," Edward B. Eastwick, op. cit., p. 103.

44 Cf. R.P. Anderson, "It seems advisable to me that I should prepare a place for you in the city," op. cit., p. 199.

45 ". . . the nobles said, 'to oblige the King, the proper course is for thee to come into the city for a few days and learn the nature of the place; after which, if the serenity of thy precious time suffers disturbance from the society of others, thou wilt be still free to choose," Edward B. Eastwick, op. cit., p. 103, and Francis Gladwin, "The ministers of state said, 'It is necessary for the satisfaction of his majesty that you should remove into the city for a few days, to make an experiment of the nature of the place, when if you should find your precious time disturbed by the society of the others, the choice will still remain in your power," op. cit., pp. 102-3.

46 Cf. Edward B. Eastwick, ". . . the devotee entered the city and they prepared for him the garden of the King's own palace, a place delightsome to the mind and suited to tranquilise the spirit," op. cit., p. 103.

47 *Like beauty's cheek, bright shone its roses red;*
Its hyacinths — like fair ones' ringlets spread
Seemed babes, which from their mother's milk ne'er drew,
In winter's cold so shrinkingly they grew.
Edward B. Eastwick, op. cit., p. 103. R.P. Anderson has given an interesting interpretation, calling this the most beautiful simile in the entire Gulistan. "The nurse here alluded is Dame Nature, and the fresh and brilliant appearance of the winter sun, when rising in all its grandeur over the snowclad mountains, is elegantly compared to the sprightly look of a new-born babe, whose first desire, on entering the world is for milk. The mountains are often dominated Nurse Nature's breasts, and the snow being melted by the rays of the sun, suggests the pretty idea of its being that orb's nutriment which it seems to suck up (i.e. to melt) immediately on rising (i.e. on coming to the world)," op. cit., p. 199.

48 *And the branches on them grew pomegranate flowers*
Like fire, suspended there, 'mid verdant bowers.
Edward B. Eastwick, op. cit., p. 103. Cf. Francis Gladwin, ". . . the branches of the trees were ornamented with scarlet flowers, suspended amongst verdant foliage, shining like fire . . ." op. cit., p. 103.

49 *A young moon that e'en saints might lead astray,*
Angel in form, a peacock in display,

When once beheld, not hermits could retain
Their holy state, nor undisturbed remain.
Edward B. Eastwick, op. cit., p. 104. Cf. Francis Gladwin, ". . . would fascinate an anchorite; and her angelic form, arrayed in all the peacock's pride and splendour, would at first view deprive the most rigid moralist of the command of his passions," op. cit., p. 103.

50 Edward B. Eastwick is concise, ". . . In the like manner, after her, the King sent a slave, a youth of rare beauty and of graceful proportions," op. cit., p. 104. Cf. Francis Gladwin, ". . . a youth of rare beauty and most exquisite symmetry of form. . . ." op. cit., p. 103.

51 *Round him, who seems cupbearer, people sink;*
Of thirst they die, he gives them not to drink.
The eyes that see him, still unsated crave,
As dropsy thirsts amid the Euphrates' waves.
Edward B. Eastwick, op. cit., p. 104. Cf. Francis Gladwin, ". . . the eyes could not be satisfied with the sight of him, like one afflicted with the dropsy beholding the Euphrates . . . ," op. cit., p. 104.

52 Cf. Edward B. Eastwick, ". . . the ringlets of the beautiful are the fetters of reason, and a snare to the bird of intelligence," op. cit., p. 104.

53 Francis Gladwin, ". . . In your service, I have lost my heart, my religion, and my reason. . . ." op. cit., p. 104.

54 *In the behoof, my heart, my faith, my intellect, I vow;*
In truth a subtle bird am I; the snare this day art thou.
Edward B. Eastwick, op. cit., p. 104. Cf. Francis Gladwin, ". . . in truth, I am now the bird of wisdom, and you are the snare . . ." op. cit., p. 104.

55 *All that exist — disciples, doctors, saints,*
The pure and eloquent alike, all fail
When once this world's base gear their mind attaints,
As flies their legs in honey vainly trail.
Edward B. Eastwick, op. cit., p. 104. Cf. Francis Gladwin, "To be brief, his state of enjoyment began to decline, in the manner as has been said, 'whenever a lawyer, a teacher, a disciple, or an orator, possessed of pure spirit, descends to mean worldly concernments, he will find himself enthralled, like flies with their feet in honey," op. cit., p. 104.

56 Cf. R.P. Anderson, ". . . reclining on a pillow of Damask silk . . . ," op. cit., p. 203.

57 Cf. Edward B. Eastwick, "Of all the people in the world, I value these two sorts the most — the learned and the devout," op. cit., p. 105. Francis Gladwin, "I have an affection for two descriptions of men in the world, the learned, and the recluse," op. cit., p. 105.

58 *To devout, nor pence nor gold divide;*
If one receives it, seek another guide.
Edward B. Eastwick, op. cit., p. 105. Cf. Francis Gladwin, ". . . the law of benevolence requires that you should do good to both of them; give money to the learned, that

others may be induced to study; but give nothing to recluses, in order that they may continue such," op. cit., p. 105.

59 *Kind manners and a heart on God bestowed*
Make up the saint, without alms begged or bread.
Edward B. Eastwick, op. cit., p. 105. Cf. Francis Gladwin, "Whosoever possesseth a virtuous disposition, and has his mind devoted to God, is a religious man, without feeding on consecrated bread, or begging for broken rituals," op. cit., p. 105.

60 "The finger of a beautiful woman, and the tip of her ear are handsome, without an ear jewel or a turquoise ring," R.P. Anderson, op. cit., p. 205.

61 "He is a durwaish who is virtuous and wise although he tasteth not holy bread, nor the fragments of beggary," R.P. Anderson, op. cit., p. 205.

62 Francis Gladwin, "The lady endowed with an elegant form and a beautiful face is charming without paint or jewelry," op. cit., p. 105.

63 *Seek I for goods which not to me belong;*
Then if men call me wordly they are not wrong.
Edward B. Eastwick, op. cit., p. 105. Cf. Francis Gladwin, "Whilst I have any thing of my own, and covet the goods of others, if you do not call me a religious man, perhaps you will not be mistaken." op. cit., pp. 105-6.

64 Cf. Edward B. Eastwick, "One of the Syrian recluses had for years worshipped in the desert, and sustained life by feeding on the leaves of trees. The King of that region made a pilgrimage to visit him, and said, 'If thou thinkest fit . . .,' " op. cit., p. 103.

65 Cf. Edward B. Eastwick, (the King) ". . . found the recluse altered in appearance from what he was before, with a florid complexion, and waxen fat, pillowed on a cushion of brocade, and the fairy faced slave standing at his head, with a fan of peacock's feathers," op. cit., p. 104.

66 James Ross, op. cit., pp. 186-98.

67 "They tell a story of a wrestler . . . ," Francis Gladwin, op. cit., p. 149.

68 *Merit and skill are weak while in husk*
Aloes they cast on fire, and crush down musk.
Edward B. Eastwick, op. cit., p. 136. Cf. Francis Gladwin, "Talents and skill are of no value without being exhibited; they put lignum aloes on fire and rub musk," op. cit., p. 149.

69 "The father said, O son! Put out of thy head this impracticable idea, and draw the feet of contentment under the skirt of security: as the wise have said, 'Riches are not to be gained by exertion; the best resource is the chagrin oneself less," Edward B. Eastwick, op. cit., p. 136. Cf. Francis Gladwin, "Riches are not to be obtained by bodily exertion, but remedy against want is to moderate our desires," op. cit., p. 150.

70 "If every hair of your head possessed two hundred accomplishments, they would be of no use when fortune is unpropitious." Francis Gladwin, op. cit., p. 150.

71 *No one by strength of arm can fortune find*
'Tis labour lost — collyrium for the blind.

Hast thou hundred virtues on each hair?
With adverse faith thou still wilt badly fare.
What can th'ill-starred athlete do? How thrive?
Can he, though strong, with stronger fortune survive?
Edward B. Eastwick, op. cit., pp. 136-7. Cf. Francis Gladwin, ". . . the arm of fortune is better than the arm of strength," op. cit., p. 150.

72 ". . . the advantages of travelling are many, the recreation of mind, profitable attainments, to see wonders, and to hear strange things; the view of cities; the conversation of mankind, the acquisition of honour, and attainment of manners; the increase of wealth, the means of gaining a livelihood, forming intimate connections, and the experience of the world . . . ," Francis Gladwin, op. cit., p. 150.

73 *Whilst thou art wedded to thy shop and home,*
O simpleton! A man thou ne'er wilt be;
Go blithely forth, and in the wide world roam,
Ere thou roam'st from it to eternity.
Edward B. Eastwick, op. cit., p. 137. Cf. Francis Gladwin, ". . . As long as you stick to your shop, and to your house, never, O simpleton, will you become a man. Go and travel over the world, before the time shall arrive for your quitting it," op. cit., p. 150.

74 ". . . the advantage of travel in the manner thou has mentioned is great; but it is secured to five kinds of persons," Edward B. Eastwick, op. cit., p. 137.

75 ". . . The merchant, who possessing wealth and dignity, with beautiful slaves and handmaids and active servants, may pass everyday in a new city, and every night in a different place, and may every minute in a delightful spots recreate himself with wordly luxuries . . . ," Francis Gladwin, op. cit., p. 150.

76 *In the mountain-waste, or forest wild, the rich man is not strange;*
Where'er he goes his tent is pitched, and there his court is made.
But he who has not this world's gear must ever friendless range,
Nor even in his fatherland will comfort find nor aid.
Edward B. Eastwick, op. cit., p. 137.

77 ". . . the learned man from whose sweetness of speech, and power of language, and stock of eloquence, wherever he goes, all hasted to serve him . . . ," Edward B. Eastwick, op. cit., p. 137.

78 Cf. Francis Gladwin, ". . . The presence of wise man resembles pure gold, because withersoever he goeth, they know his intrinsic value and consequence," op. cit., p. 150.

79 *The wise man's nature is like purest gold:*
Where'er he comes all know his value, prize his worth.
But men will, cheap as leathern money, hold
The witless lord, save in the land that gave him birth.
Edward B. Eastwick, op. cit., p. 138.

80 Cf. Francis Gladwin, ". . . The beautiful person, to whom the heart of the virtuous are inclined, set a high value on his company, and consider it an honour to do him service," op. cit., p. 151.

81 "A little beauty is better than much wealth: a fair countenance is a salve for heart sickness, and the key of closed doors," Edward B. Eastwick, op. cit., p. 138.

82 *Let beauty travel where it will, it finds respectful greeting,*
Though its won parents, wrathfully, should drive it from its home.
One day, amid the Kuran's leaves, a peacock's feather meeting,
I said, 'This place exceeds thy worth, thou dost it not become.'
'Peace!' it replied, for to each one who wears the charm of beauty,
Go where he will, all him receive with favour as a duty.
Edward B. Eastwick, op. cit., p. 138.

83 Cf. Francis Gladwin, ". . . the son who is endowed with elegance and beauty, careth not for his father's anger," op. cit., p. 152.

84 *When the son beauty has, and courtesy,*
Let him not care how could his sire be.
He is a pearl, what if the shell be lost?
Who for a priceless pearl will grudge the cost?
Edward B. Eastwick, op. cit., pp. 138-9.

85 ". . . he who possesses a sweet voice; who, with the throat of David, retrains the water from flowing, and arrests the bird in flight; and moreover, by means of his excellence, captivates the hearts of men, and spiritual persons eagerly desire his companionship," Edward B. Eastwick, op. cit., p. 138. Cf. Francis Gladwin, ". . . a sweet singer who with the throat of David arrests the water in their course, and suspends the birds in their flight; consequently, by the power of this perfection, he captivates the hearts of the mankind in general, and the religious are desirous of associating with him. My attention is engaged in listening to a sweet voice: who is this beautiful person playing on the double chord?", op. cit., p. 153.

86 *My ears attend his melody;*
Who's this whose hands the lute-strings try How winningly a soft and tender voice
Comes to the ears of friends, whom th'early bowl
Makes blithe! in it, more than in looks, rejoice
All hearts; these the sense gladden: that the soul.
Edward B. Eastwick, op. cit., p. 139.

87 ". . . the artisan, who gains the means of support by the labour of his arm, so that his character is not jeopardized for bread . . . ," Edward B. Eastwick, op. cit., p. 138.

88 Cf. Francis Gladwin, ". . . the king of Neemroze . . .", op. cit., p. 153.

89 *If want from his own city should expel*
A cotton carder, he'd not feel distress;
But if the king of Nimroz, ruined, fell
From his high place, he'd slumber supperless.
Edward B. Eastwick, op. cit., p. 138.

90 Cf. Francis Gladwin, "The abovementioned qualities, which I have explained, are the means of affording comfort to the mind in travelling, and are the bestowers of sweet

delight; but he who does not possess them, will enter the world with vain expectations and no one will hear his name, nor see any signs of him," op. cit., p. 153.

91 *He, whom t'afflict uprisings revolving fate*
Malevolent, is led by destiny
Against his will. The pegion, who his mate
Shall ne'er revisit, follows fate's decree
Towards the net.
Edward B. Eastwick, op. cit., p. 140.

92 The son said, O father! How can I contradict another maxim of the sages which says, "The necessaries of life are distributed to all, yet the attainment thereof requires exertion, and although misfortune is decreed, it is our duty to shun the way by which it enters," Francis Gladwin, op. cit., p. 154.

93 *Though, without doubt, fate will want our supply,*
Reason requires it be sought from home
'Tis true that none will unpredestined die,
Yet in a dragon's maw one should not come.
Edward B. Eastwick, op. cit., p. 140.

94 "In my present situation I am able to encounter a furious elephant, and to combat a devouring lion; and I have besides this inducement to travel, that I am no longer to suffer indigence," Francis Gladwin, op. cit., p. 154.

95 *Whene'er a man from home and country flies*
All earth is his; he has no further care.
Each night the rich man to his place hies:
Where night descends, the poor man's home is there.
Edward B. Eastwick, op. cit., p. 140. Cf. Francis Gladwin, "When a man falls from his rank and dignity, what has he more to concern about? He is a citizen of the world. A rich man repairs at night to his palace, but wheresoever the Durwaish is overtaken by night, that place is his inn," op. cit., p. 154.

96 *The man of worth, whose fate is cross, will go*
Where men have never learned his name to know.
Edward B. Eastwick, op. cit., p. 140.

97 "He travelled until he arrived on the banks of a river, so rapid that stones dashed against stones, and the noise was heard at many miles distance. It was a tremendous water, in which even water fowls were not in safety; and the smallest of its waves would impel a millstone from the shore," Francis Gladwin, op. cit., p. 155.

98 *A stream so dread, not birds were safe amid its waters' roar;*
The smallest of its waves would sweep a mill-stone from its shore.
Edward B. Eastwick, op. cit., p. 141.

99 "He saw a number of people sitting at the ferry, each of whom had a small piece of money, and they were making up their bundles for the passage," Francis Gladwin, op. cit., p. 155.

100 *Thou canst not make any strength of arm the want of gold supply;*
And hast thou gold, thou needst not to threaten or defy.
Edward B. Eastwick, op. cit., p. 141.

101 Francis Gladwin, "The inhuman boatman laughed at him, and turned away, saying . . ." op. cit., p. 155.

102 *Gold thou hast not; the passage o'er by force may not be won;*
What is the strength of ten men here? Bring thou the gold for one.
Edward B. Eastwick, op. cit., p. 141.

103 "The young man, incensed at this sarcasm, wished to be revenged on him. The boat had put off; he called out, 'If you will be satisfied with this garment, which I have on my back, I will freely give it to you.' The boatman being greedy, brought back the boat . . . ," Francis Gladwin, op. cit., p. 155.

104 *The eyes of men, though sharp, are closed by avarice;*
Greed will both bird and fish towards the net entice.
Edward B. Eastwick, op. cit., p. 142.

105 ". . . When you see fighting, be peaceable, for a peaceable disposition shuts the door of contentment. Oppose kindness to perverseness; the sharp sword will not cut soft silk . . . ," Francis Gladwin, op. cit., p. 156.

106 *Act thou forbearingly when discord's rife,*
For gentleness will close the gates of strife.
When thou seest broils arise, use courtesy;
A sharp sword cuts not silk, though soft it be.
With honeyed words, good humour on thy side,
Thou, with a hair, and elephant mayst guide.
Edward B. Eastwick, op. cit., p. 142.

107 "The young man in the vanity of his strength, of which he had boasted, thoughtless of the offended heart of his enemy, paid no attention to this maxim of sages . . . ," Francis Gladwin, op. cit., pp. 156-7.

108 *Fancy not thyself safe, for thou shalt moan,*
Who hast another treated cruelly.
Against the castle-wall hurl not a stone,
Lest from the walls a stone descend on thee.
Edward B. Eastwick, op. cit., p. 143.

109 ". . . the third day sleep overpowered him and flang him into the river . . . ," Francis Gladwin, op. cit., p. 157.

110 *Gnats will an elephant o'ercome, if they*
Unite against their foe, so huge and grim.
And ants collected in one dense array,
Though fierce the lion be, will vanquish him.
Edward B. Eastwick, op. cit., p. 144.

111 "Sick and wounded, he fell in with a caravan, which from necessity he followed," Francis Gladwin, op. cit., p. 158.

112 "The cravings of the young man's appetite being very powerful, he eat and drank so much, that at length the inner demon was quieted, and being overpowered with fatigue, he fell asleep," Francis Gladwin, op. cit., p. 159.

113 *With a companion I ne'er felt secure*
Until I learned his inward qualities.
Wounds from a foeman's tooth are worse t' endure
When he has shown himself in friendship's guise.
Edward B. Eastwick, op. cit., p. 145.

114 Cf. Francis Gladwin, "A traveller has no friends besides a traveller," op. cit., p. 160.

115 *Gone are the yellow camels now: who will address me more?*
The poor man has no comrade – no comrade but poor.
With poor wanderer they will harshly deal
Who ne'er experienced what the friendless feel.
Edward B. Eastwick, op. cit., p. 146.

116 ". . . the king's son, compassionating him, bestowed on him a garment and money, and ordered a trusty person to accompany him, and see him safe to his own city," Francis Gladwin, op. cit., p. 161.

117 *That needy gladiator said right well,*
A grain of gold doth pounds of strength excel.
Edward B. Eastwick, op. cit., p. 146.

118 ". . . Don't you perceive that, in return for the little distress that I suffered, how much wealth I have brought with me; and for the sting that I endured, what a stock of honey I have acquired?", Francis Gladwin, op. cit., pp. 161-2.

119 *Tough more than fate supplies we ne'er can gain,*
Yet must we strive that portion to obtain
From the revening moster's jaw, should the diver pause and gasp,
He'd never hold the precious pearl, the bright pearl in his grasp,
The lower mill-stone revolves not, and hence
Of necessity supports the greater burthen
On what would savage lions feed? If they
In their deep dens abode. The hawk would win
Small sustenance did it ne'er seek its prey.
And, like a spider's, will thy limbs grow thin,
If thine own house alone thou huntest in.
Edward B. Eastwick, op. cit., p. 147. Cf. Francis Gladwin, ". . . Although we cannot enjoy more than Providence has assigned us, we ought not to be negligent in acquiring it. If the diver were to think of the jaw of crocodile, it would never get in its possession precious pearls. The lower millstone does not move, and therefore sustains a great weight. What food can a ravenous lion find in his den? What game can be taken by a

hawk that cannot fly? If you wait in your house for provision, your hands and feet will become as thin as those of a spider . . . ," op. cit., p. 162.

120 *The hunter does not always win the prey,*
Perchance a tiger may rend him one day.
Edward B. Eastwick, op. cit., p. 148.

121 *The sage whose bright mind mirrors truth,*
May sometimes wander wide of it:
While, by mistake, the simple youth,
Will, with his shaft, the target hit.
Edward B. Eastwick, op. cit., p. 148. Cf. Francis Gladwin, ". . . After this the boy burnt his bow and arrows, and on their asking him, why he had done so, he replied, 'that this my first repute may be lasting'. It may happen that the prudent counsel of the enlightened sage does not succeed; and it may chance that an unskillful boy, through mistake, hits the mark with his arrow," op. cit., p. 163.

122 ". . . The young man was incensed at this sarcasm, and burned to revenge himself upon it. . . ." Edward B. Eastwick, op. cit., pp. 141-2.

123 ". . . and looking on his form, he saw that his external shape was comely, while his appearance betokened wretchedness. He asked him whence he was, and how he had come there?" Edward B. Eastwick, op. cit., p. 146.

124 James Ross, op. cit., pp. 210-12.

125 "When your sweetheart will not look at your gold, that metal and earth appear alike in your sight," Francis Gladwin, op. cit., p. 181.

126 "His friends besought him to relinquish this vain imagination, many besides himself being seized with this hope," Francis Gladwin, op. cit., p. 181.

127 ". . . warriors kill their enemies by the strength of their hands and shoulders; but those who are beautiful, destroy their friends," Francis Gladwin, op. cit., p. 181.

128 "I persist, because no other course remains, even though my adversary covers me with wounds from a sword, or an arrow. If I should be able, I will seize her sleeve, otherwise I will go and expire at her threshold," Francis Gladwin, op. cit., p. 181.

129 "His relations, who wished him well, and pitied his condition, administered advice; and fettered him without any benefit," Francis Gladwin, op. cit., p. 181.

130 Francis Gladwin, has translated as "king's son", op. cit., p. 182.

131 Cf. Francis Gladwin, "The Prince, who knew himself to be the object of the young man's attachment, and that he had raised this dust of calamity, galloped his horse towards him," op. cit., p. 182.

132 Cf. Francis Gladwin, "Notwithstanding, the Prince shewed him great kindness; and asked from whence come you, what is your name, and what profession to you follow. The youth was so immersed in the profundity of friendship and attachment that absolutely he was not able to utter a word," op. cit., pp. 182-3.

133 "Although you know the seven portions of Koran by heart, when you become distracted with love, you will not remember your alphabet," Francis Gladwin, op. cit., p. 183.

134 "It is wonderful how I can exist, when admitted to your presence; and that having heard your voice, I should be able to reply," Francis Gladwin, op. cit., p. 183.

135 "It would not be surprising if one should be killed at the gate of his beloved, but it would be astonishing if he came there alive, and brought back his soul in safety," Francis Gladwin, op. cit., p. 183.

136 James Ross, op. cit., pp. 221-2.

137 Cf. Francis Gladwin, "I recollect that in my youth as I was passing through a street, I cast my eyes on a beautiful girl. It was in the autumn, when the heat had dried up all the moisture from the mouth, and the sultry wind made the marrow boil in the bones . . . ," op. cit., p. 197.

138 ". . . in so much that it seemed as if the dawn was rising in the obscurity of night, or as if the water of immortality was issuing from the land of darkness. . . . ," Francis Gladwin, op. cit., pp. 197-8.

139 ". . . The thirst of my heart cannot be slaked with a drop of water, nor if I should drink rivers would it be lessened," Edward B. Eastwick, op. cit., p. 165. Cf. Francis Gladwin, ". . . The thirst of my heart is not such that it can be allayed with a drop of pure water, the streams of whole river would not satisfy it . . . ," op. cit., p. 198.

140 *Most blest that happy one whose gaze intense*
Rests on such face at each successive morn;
The drunk with wine at midnight may sense
Regain; but not till the last day shall dawn
Will love's intoxication reach its bourne.

Edward B. Eastwick, op. cit., p. 165. Cf. Francis Gladwin, ". . . How happy is that fortunate person whose eyes every morning may behold such a countenance. He who is intoxicated with wine will be sober again in the course of the night; but he who is intoxicated by the cupbearer, will not recover his senses until the day of judgement . . . ," op. cit., p. 198.

141 ". . . or as the waters of life issuing from the gloom. She held in her hand a cup of snow-water, in which she had mixed sugar and the juice of grape. I know not whether she had perfumed it . . . ," Edward B. Eastwick, op. cit., p. 165.

142 James Ross, op. cit., pp. 228-34.

143 "That stately cypress coming into my sight has captivated my heart and deprived me of my strength, so that I prostrate at her feet. Those mischievous eyes drew my heart into the snare. If you wish to preserve your heart, shut your eyes. I cannot by any means get her out of my thought: I am the snake with the bruised head; I cannot turn myself," Francis Gladwin, op. cit., p. 206.

144 "The cazy said to the respectable man of learning who was in his company, 'behold that beauteous girl how rude she is; behold her arched eyebrow, what a sweet frown it exhibits! In Arabic they say that a blow from the hand of her we love, is as sweet as raisins. To receive a blow on the mouth from thy hand, is preferable to eating bread from one's own hand,' " Francis Gladwin, op. cit., pp. 206-7.

145 "Unripe grapes are sour, but keep them a day or two and they will become sweet," Francis Gladwin, op. cit., p. 207.

146 ". . . That with permission they would represent a matter to him. . . . Although . . . it is criminal to describe the faults of a great personage," Francis Gladwin, op. cit., p. 207.

147 "The laws of rectitude require that you should conquer this inclination, and not give way to unlawful desires," Francis Gladwin, op. cit., pp. 207-8.

148 "You are acquainted with your mistresses' character, and have heard her conversation," Francis Gladwin, op. cit., p. 208.

149 ". . . The advice which my friends have given, in regard to my situation, is perfectly right, and their arguments are unanswerable . . . ," Francis Gladwin, op. cit., p. 208.

150 Gladwin has not included this sentence in his translation.

151 "He who has money in the scales has strength in his arms; and he who has not the command of money, is destitute of friends in the world," Francis Gladwin, op. cit., p. 208.

152 ". . . one night he obtained a meeting in private, and the superintendent of the police was immediately informed of the circumstance, that the Cazi had passed the whole night in drinking wine, and fondling his mistress. He was too happy to sleep and was singing . . . ," Francis Gladwin, op. cit., p. 209.

153 "In that instant, when the eye of enmity is asleep, be thou upon the watch, lest some mischance befall you . . . ," Francis Gladwin, op. cit., p. 209.

154 ". . . until you hear the mouzzin proclaiming the hour of prayer; or the sound of the kettle drum from the gate of the police of Atabuk, it would be foolishness to cease kissing at the crowning of the foolish cock," Francis Gladwin, op. cit., p. 209.

155 ". . . your enemies have laid snare for you; nay they have said the truth . . . , " Francis Gladwin, op. cit., p. 209.

156 ". . . If the lion has his paw on the game, what signifies it if the dog should come. Turn your face towards your mistress, and let your rival bite the back of his hand . . . ," Francis Gladwin, op. cit., p. 210.

157 ". . . He saw the candle burning, and the mistress sitting down, with the wine spilt, and the glass broken; and the Cazy stupified between sleep and intoxication, lost to all sense of his existence . . . ," Francis Gladwin, op. cit., pp. 210-11.

158 ". . . If you seize me, I deserve it, but if you pardon me, forgiveness is better than vengeance . . . ," Francis Gladwin, op. cit., p. 211.

159 ". . . Repentances can now avail nothing, as you know that you are about to suffer death. What good is there in a thief's repentance, when he has not the power of throwing a rope into the upper story? Tell him who is tall not to pluck the fruit, for he of low stature cannot extend his arm to the branch. To you who have been convicted of such wickedness, there can be no hopes of escape . . . ," Francis Gladwin, op. cit., p. 211.

160 ". . . As long as I labour under your displeasure, think not that I will let go the skirt of your garment. Although the crime which I have committed may be unpardonable, still I entertain some hopes from your clemency . . . ," Francis Gladwin, op. cit., p. 212.

161 "... O monarch of universe, I have been fostered in your family, and am not singular in commission of such crimes, therefore I beseech you to precipitate someone else, in order that I may benefit by the example ...," Francis Gladwin, op. cit., p. 212.

162 "... All of you are burthened with defects of your own, reproach not others with their failings. Whosoever is sensible of his own faults carps not at another's failing," Francis Gladwin, op. cit., p. 212.

163 James Ross, op. cit., pp. 260-71.

164 "I saw sitting in a company, a certain person who wore the habit of a Durwaish, but without possessing the disposition of one, and being inclined to be querulous, he had opened the book of complaint, and began censuring the rich," Francis Gladwin, op. cit., p. 245.

165 *The merciful are ever moneyless;*
Hardhearted they who have power to bless.
Edward B. Eastwick, op. cit., p. 193.

166 "... the rich are the revenue of the poor, a storehouse for the recluse, the pilgrim's hope, and the asylum of travellers. They are the bearers of burthens for the relief of others," Francis Gladwin, op. cit., p. 246.

167 *Offerings to God, bequests to furnish ease*
To the worn traveller, enfranchisement
Of slaves, alms, gifts and sacrifices — these
Are rich men's works. Say, when wilt thou invent
Like merits for thyself, who canst but pray,
With twice a hundred wanderings, twice a day.
Edward B. Eastwick, op. cit., p. 194.

168 "The rich perform both moral and religious duties, in the most perfect manner, because they possess wealth, out of which they bestow alms; their garments are clan, and their reputation spotless, with minds void of care," Francis Gladwin, op. cit., pp. 246-7.

169 "For what strength can be with an empty stomach? What bounty from an empty hand? How can the fettered feet walk? And from the hungry belly what munificence can be expected?" Francis Gladwin, op. cit., p. 247.

170 *The man at night uneasy sleeps,*
Who knows not how to gain tomorrow's bread:
The ant in summer corn upheaps;
'Tis thus in winter with abundance fed.
Edward B. Eastwick, op. cit., p. 194.

171 "Leisure and poverty are not found together, and satisfaction dwelleth not with distress. One is standing up to evening prayers, whilst the other is sitting down wishing for his supper. How can the two be compared?" Francis Gladwin, op. cit., p. 247.

172 *The rich man is with thoughts of God impressed:*
The needy is for such thoughts too distressed.
Edward B. Eastwick, op. cit., p. 195.

173 "The Arabians say, God defend me from humiliating poverty, and from the neighbourhood of one I do not love." Edward B. Eastwick, op. cit., p. 195.

174 "Poverty blackens the countenance in both worlds," Edward B. Eastwick, op. cit., p. 195.

175 *O noisy drum, all emptiness within,*
How without food wilt thou thy march begin!
Be manly, and from cringing cease: for this
Than thousand-beaded rosaries better is.
Edward B. Eastwick, op. cit., p. 195.

176 "A Durwaish without a vital religion, will not rest until his poverty ends in blasphemy," Francis Gladwin, op. cit., p. 248.

177 "Poverty borders on the denial of God," Edward B. Eastwick, op. cit., p. 196.

178 "Without the command of riches, you cannot clothe the naked, nor use means for liberating captives: How can such as ourselves attain to their dignity, and what comparison is there between the hand that bestows and that which receives?" Francis Gladwin, op. cit., p. 248.

179 "To them these is an assured allowance of fruits, and they are honoured in the gardens of Paradise," Edward B. Eastwick, op. cit., p. 196.

180 *To those athirst the whole world seems*
A spring of water in their dreams.
Edward B. Eastwick, op. cit., p. 196.

181 "You will everywhere see a person who is in distress commit atrocious actions without any hesitation; not being deterred by the dread of future punishment, he discriminates not between lawful and unlawful," Francis Gladwin, op. cit., p. 248.

182 *A dog leaps up with joy when on his head*
A clod descends — he thinks a bone to spy.
So, when two men bear forth the coffined dead
Upon their shoulders, greedy miscreants eye
The bier, and think they then a tray of meat descry.
Edward B. Eastwick, op. cit., p. 196.

183 ". . . the rich man, whom God hath regarded with the eye of favour, by the performance of what is lawful, is preserved from the commission of what is illegal," Francis Gladwin, op. cit., p. 249.

184 Cf. Francis Gladwin, "And it is possible that the Durwaish, at the instigation of lust, not having power to restrain it, may commit sin . . . ," op. cit., p. 250.

185 *Her hands in gore of hapless lovers dipped,*
Her fingers with the ruddy jujube tipped.
Edward B. Eastwick, op. cit., p. 197.

186 *A heart that Houris charmed and made its prey,*
To Yaghma's beauties when will devious stray.
Edward B. Eastwick, op. cit., p. 198.

187 *Who holds the dates he loves his hands between,*
Contended, pelts the clusters not, I ween.
Edward B. Eastwick, op. cit., p. 198.

188 ". . . . those in indigent circumstances want chastity; as those who are starving steal bread . . . ," Francis Gladwin, op. cit., p. 250.

189 *So when a raveneous cur finds meat — small care has he*
If Salih's camel or if Dajjal's ass it be.
Edward B. Eastwick, op. cit., p. 198.

190 "Many decent persons have fallen into abominable wickedness through poverty, and have given their precious honour to the winds of disgrace," Edward B. Eastwick, op. cit., p. 198.

191 *With hunger abstinence will scarce remain,*
And want will wrest away devotion's rein.
Edward B. Eastwick, op. cit., p. 198. Cf. Francis Gladwin, "Amidst the cravings of hunger, the power of abstaining ceases, poverty snatcheth the reins out of the hand of piety," op. cit., p. 250.

192 "At the moment that I uttered these words, the Durwaish's patience being exhausted, he attacked me with all the vehemence and loquacity . . . ," Francis Gladwin, op. cit., p. 250.

193 *When a fool would exalt himself, for his wealth, above the wise,*
Though he be an ox of ambergris, him as a foll despise.
Edward B. Eastwick, op. cit., p. 199.

194 ". . . Speak not disdainfully of them, as they are masters of generosity . . . ," Francis Gladwin, op. cit., p. 251.

195 ". . . They stir not a step in the service of God, and part not with a direm without distressing you with the obligation. They labor in amassing wealth, preserve it with avarice, and part it with regret, verifying the saying of the sages that 'the miser's money comes out of the earth, at the time that he goes into it' . . . ," Francis Gladwin, op. cit., p. 252.

196 *With toil and trouble one does riches gain,*
Another comes and reaps them without pain.
Edward B. Eastwick, op. cit., p. 200.

197 ". . . You know nothing of the parsimony of the wealthy excepting by means of beggary; for otherwise, whosoever lays aside avarice sees no difference between the bountiful man and the miser . . . ," Francis Gladwin, op. cit., p. 252.

198 *The soulless, stingy, dull, and senseless wight,*
Bids thee go say, 'There's no one in,' — he's right!
Edward B. Eastwick, op. cit., p. 200. Cf. Francis Gladwin, ". . . he who hath neither wisdom, liberality, prudence, nor judgment, of him the porter says rightly, that no one is in the house . . . ," op. cit., p. 253.

199 *No wealth could fill the eyes of avarice,*
As dew to brim a well would ne'er suffice.
Edward B. Eastwick, op. cit., p. 201.

200 ". . . their riches," Francis Gladwin, op. cit., p. 253.

201 ". . . we were talking thus, opposing force to force . . . ," Francis Gladwin, op. cit., p. 253.

202 ". . . take care not to throw down the shield when combating with an orator, who hath nothing but borrowed tumid eloquence . . . ," Francis Gladwin, op. cit., p. 254.

203 *Beware, lest at the speaker's onset, who*
Has but a borrowed and a vain tirade,
Thou should'st thy shield fling down.
Keep thyself true
To faith and virtue, and be not afraid
Of empty posts with arms above the doors displayed.
Edward B. Eastwick, op. cit., p. 201.

204 ". . . It is the way with the ignorant, when confounded by the adversaries arguments, to have recourse to violence . . . ," Francis Gladwin, op. cit., p. 254.

205 *O'er him I tumbled, he o'er me,*
A crowd with laughter us pursued,
And wondered at our colloquy
With fingers in their mouths fast glued.
Edward B. Eastwick, op. cit., p. 202.

206 "O thou who hast spoken in praise of the rich, I would have thee to know that there is no rose without a thorn; and that wine is accompanied with intoxication; hidden treasure has its dragon; in some place which has royal pearls, are ravenous crocodiles; the enjoyment of worldly pleasure is followed by the sting of death; and the lights of paradise are intercepted by crafty Satan," Francis Gladwin, op. cit., p. 255.

207 *Who would have friends, a foe's hate must sustain,*
Linked are snakes, gold; thorns, flowers; joy and pain.
Edward B. Eastwick, op. cit., p. 202.

208 ". . . Observe you not that in the garden there are odoriferous plants, as well as dry trunks? In the like manner in the circle of rich men, there are grateful and ungrateful persons; and in number of Durwaishes some exercise patience, and others do not . . . ," Francis Gladwin, op. cit., p. 255.

209 *Could every hailstone to a pearl be turned,*
Pearls in the mart like oyster shells were spurned.
Edward B. Eastwick, op. cit., p. 203.

210 ". . . The beloved of the Almighty consist of rich men, who have the disposition of Durwaishes, and of Durwaishes possessed of noble minds . . . ," Francis Gladwin, op. cit., p. 256.

211 *What though another die of want? my bread*
Fails not: to water-fowls floods cause no dread.
Edward B. Eastwick, op. cit., p. 203.

212 *Borne aloft in camel-litters, what, I pray, do women care*
For the tired pilgrim struggling through the sand-heaps drifted there?
Edward B. Eastwick, op. cit., p. 203.

213 *The base who've saved their own vile wrappers cry,*
'What matters though the universe should die?'
Edward B. Eastwick, op. cit., p. 203.

214 ". . . I have seen others who having spread the table of generosity and proclaimed munificence, with affable countenance seek reputation, and ask pardon of God; enjoying the things of this world and of futurity . . . ," Francis Gladwin, op. cit., p. 257.

215 *No sire e'er showed such kindness to his child*
As thy all-bounteous hand hath heaped on man.
Heaven on this world with favouring mercy smiled,
And by its Providence thy reign began.
Edward B. Eastwick, op. cit., p. 204. Cf. Francis Gladwin, "A father sheweth not such benevolence towards his son, as your hand of liberality bestowed on the human race. God wanting to bestow a blessing on mankind through His mercy made you the King of world," op. cit., p. 257.

216 ". . . We took the road of affability . . . ," Francis Gladwin, op. cit., p. 257.

217 *Complain not, darwesh! of vicissitude:*
Hapless if in such train of thought thou die!
And thou, rich man! While yet thou art endued
With a kind heart and riches, gratify
Thyself and others: thus on earth make sure
Of joys; and thy reward in heaven secure.
Edward B. Eastwick, op. cit., p. 204. Cf. Francis Gladwin, " . . . that thou mayest obtain the blessing of heaven, in this life and in futurity," op. cit., p. 258.

218 ". . . but there is another numerous body who prepare a hospitable table and proclaim a liberal invitation, and whose countenances expand with affability while they in this manner pursue the path of fame and divine acceptance, and thus enjoy both this present world and a future recompense . . . ," Edward B. Eastwick, op. cit., p. 204.

Appendix

SHAIKH SADI

THIRTY YEARS ago, when I first devoted myself to the study of the Oriental languages, it was my custom to translate into English any classic which my Munshi had recommended for my perusal; and, among other Persian books, I had in this way made translations of the *Gulistan* and *Bustan* of Sadi: and now, with much diffidence, publish that of the Gulistan, with an abridgment of a larger work, being an Essay on the Life and Genius of the Author, intending to follow this up next year with my translation of the Bustan, with a prefatory critique on Sadi's works, and making a volume equal in size to this; but each will otherwise be a distinct work.

Sadi has ever been with me a favourite Persian classic; and after many and diligent perusals of his Kulliat, or works, I flatter myself with having not only mastered the comparatively easy task of fully appreciating his intellectual faculties, but also the more difficult one of portraying the features and passions of his mind. In this sketch of Sadi's life I shall duly avail myself of my Asiatic authorities; as, however, Oriental notions of biography differ so essentially from ours that little is to be gleaned from them that can interest the European reader, I am fortunate in finding that anecdotes of the temper, manners, and habits of so excellent a moralist and writer are constantly occurring in his own works; and I have only to quote them to give a perfect insight into his character.

Silghur, a Turkish officer in the service of the Saljuc Sultans, usurped the government of Pars, and was the origin of that dynasty of Atabaks, or Attabegs, who reigned there A.H. 543, 668. And of them Atabak Toklah, or Toglah, reigned A.H. 571, 591, and was succeeded by his brother Atabak Saad-bin-Zungi, who reigned A.H. 591, 623, and was succeeded by his son Atabak Abubakr, A.H. 623, 658, and he again was succeeded by his son Saad-bin-Abibakr, who died within a twelvemonth, and after a few and feverish reigns of women and infants, consisting altogether of nine years, the dynasty became extinct A.H. 668; all these reigns are included within the first three-fourths of Sadi's life; but Dowlat Shah must mistake in dating Sadi's death under one of this Silghur, or Silaghur dynasty, or there must have been a second dynasty of them.

Dowlat Shah, in his *Tuzkirrah-ashshaara,* or Lives of the Persian Poets, says that Sadi's father held some office at the Shiraz court, and from what Sadi himself says, in a *Kitah,* or fragment of his book of *Sahibayah,* more immediately under the Diwan, or prime minister, speaking in eulogy of him – "My father was thy old domestic; he passed his whole life in thy service. Thy born slave, when he first saw the light, naturally cast his eyes up to thy countenance. I can never seek the patronage of another, who have been the nurtured child of thy bounty."

In the first year of Atabak Toklah's reign, or A.H. 571, A.D. 1194, Sadi was born at Shiraz, the capital of Pars, or Persia proper; and the epithet of Shirazi applies equally to him and Hafiz, as much honoured natives of that Dar u'lilom, or seat of learning. Dowlat Shah says that his proper name was Moslih u'd-din, or the Umpire of the faith; but he was better known afterwards by that of Shaikh Sadi Shirazi: Shaikh properly signifying the head of an Arabian tribe; and among Mussulmans it was anywhere conferred upon a senior, who commanded the love and esteem of his neighbours from authority, age, genius, or piety; and, on account of the two last virtues, is among the Persians more especially applied to Nizami and Sadi; and it is no small compliment that though the former is the senior and, next to Firdausi, the best Persian heroic poet, yet Sadi is appropriately called the Shaikh!

Again Sadi, or Saadi, signifying felicity, is his Tokhullus, or poetical name, and was, according to Dowlat Shah, given to him by Atabak Saad-bin-Zungi. This is probable; but he is wrong in saying that Sadi was born in that prince's reign. This mode of appellation a writer in the East does not affect till he has established his character as a poet, when, after being confirmed to him, like a title of nobility, by some sovereign prince, he takes the first opportunity of introducing his *Tokhullus* into the Shah-bayit, or last stanza of a *ghazal,* or other poem, and seldom omits to use it thus afterwards; and Cowley among ourselves has happily adopted this Oriental custom:

> The wise example of the heavenly lark,
> Thy fellow-poet, Cowley, mark;
> Above the clouds let thy proud music sound,
> Thy humble nest build on the ground !

Jami calls Sadi Sharf-u'd-din Mislah, son of Abdullah; and an Alowi, or descendant of Ali.

Sadi's father and mother were alive within his own recollection, for he often mentions the first (*Bust.* ii. 2; ix. 13, 15, etc.); and his mother, very feelingly (*Gul.* vi. 6); but, from his calling himself an orphan, both must have died while our Shaikh was yet a stripling, for he says (*Bust.* ii. 2):

> If the orphan come to cry, who will soothe him? if he be pettish, who will put up with his ill-humours? take heed, that he weep not; for the throne of the Almighty is shaken to and fro when the orphan sets a crying. Once my head was lofty, as that which wears a crown, for then I could lay it upon the bosom of a father; had a fly but dared to settle on my body, it would have been enough to alarm a whole family; but were my enemies ready to make me now their captive, none of my friends would come to my rescue: I can feel a sympathy for the helplessness of infancy, because in my childhood I lost my father.

In his Nafhat-u'l-ans, or Memoirs of the Sufis, Jami says that he was descended from the Sharif, or noble house of Abdullah Hafaif; but however dignified his birth, or lucrative his station at court, both advantages must have died with the father; otherwise we should not find Sadi using his interest with Shamsuddin to exempt his brother from some extortion in his mean occupation of retailing figs. This prime minister, then, it would seem, viceroy on the part of Abaca-an, at Shiraz, acted handsomely on the occasion by laying a thousand gold dinars at Sadi's feet, as a compensation to his brother, but would not, as the story adds, think of offering any money-compliment to a darwesh like himself. In the *Risallah*, or tract on the questions of the Lord Diwan, this same generous friend sends him five hundred *dinars* under the pretence of supplying food for his birds, of which the servant, considering himself as one of Sadi's birds, purloins a hundred and fifty, being, like the Irishman, not aware that the letter, which accompanied this gift, and its answer, would detect him. On ascertaining this knavery, the messenger is forthwith sent back with an order for Sadi on the Shiraz treasury for 10,000 gold *dinars*! And on another occasion he and his brother Ula-ud-din, joint ministers of that son and successor of the Tartar emperor, Halaku Khan, sent Sadi, then an old resident in his hermitage at Shiraz, a bag of 50,000 *dinars*, or about £24,000 of our money, which he was to lay out in building a Caravansaray under the citadel of Cohindar, near Shiraz, and which Sadi had much at heart in completing. By the mother's side Sadi's relations were some of them eminent for learning, and Mola Cut'b Alamah, his maternal uncle, is noticed as his first master in science.

Jami says that Sadi was a Sufi of profound learning, or master in every branch of science, and accomplished in the polite arts, for, according to Dowlat Shah, "he commenced his studies at the Nizamiah college of Baghdad," which, during five centuries, had been the chief seat of Oriental learning, and the magnificent residence of the Khalifs; and there he held an Idrar, or fellowship (*Bust.* vii. 14), having had for his tutor in science the learned Ab'ul Firah-ibin-Jozi (*Gul.* ii. 21), and in theology Abd-u'l-cadir the Gilani; and with the last he made his first pilgrimage to Mecca, which he repeated fourteen times, and chiefly on foot; and he often makes his adventures on such occasions the subject of an apologue (*Gul.* ii. 25, 26, etc.).

Being a classical, as well as a spoken idiom and court dialect, the Tazi, or modern Arabic, under the illustrious patronage of the Khalifs, reached as great perfection as has ever been the lot of any human tongue. Sadi knew and wrote it well, and carried the practice of deluging the Persian language with it to a greater length than any of his predecessors had done. In his *Gulistan* v. 21 he refers with fondness to its currency in A.D. 1256, at Baghdad, little thinking that in the course of two years he should have occasion to pen it in a *casidah*, or elegy, on its being sacked by Halaku the Tartar, its palaces and colleges plundered, and the Khalif Mustasim, the last of the Abissites, and all that were dignified and learned, with a million and a half of its inhabitants barbarously murdered. Sadi wrote a book of Tazi elegies; but that city and its university were his alma mater, the seat of the religion he revered, and the muses he adored; and he consequently felt a pathos on this horrible event; and all that understand it must relish its propriety and elegance.

Sadi mentions himself to have been twice married. Of his first marriage, at Aleppo, he tells a pleasant story, to which (*Gul.* ii. 30) I beg to refer the reader, desiring him to recollect that though Sadi, as a Mussulman, had like the Jews a legal right to repudiate his troublesome wife, yet, in that case, he must have repaid her dowry, and he was all his life too improvident, if not poor, to do that; besides, a sense of family honour will deter one of the orthodox from idly parting with the woman of his former affections; also he is obliged to give three notices of his intention to the Cazy; and though during the heat of passion instances occur of a first, and perhaps a second, notice, after twenty years' intercourse with them I never heard of a third, which was to complete it.

Of his other wife at Sanaa, the capital of Yamin, he makes no mention, but in *Bustan* ix. 25 laments their loss of an only son with the feelings of a parent – "If despair overwhelm thee in this abode of gloom, be wise and prepare for thyself a place of greater cheerfulness; wishest thou the night of the grave to be luminous as day, carry along with thee ready trimmed the lamp of good works." Thus could Sadi reconcile himself to a heavy loss; the duties of his religion inculcating the sin of complaining, and his philosophy teaching him that it were fruitless to repine for what he could not recall. Two such trials terrified a man of Sadi's disposition from another such connection. He thought, perhaps, like Cicero, who being, after his divorce from Tullia, invited to a second marriage, replied he could not – "*simul amare et sapare*—be wise and in love at the same time!" or, as Sadi's old friend answered, "I do not like to marry an old woman !" "Why," said his adviser, "do you not, now you are rich, choose a young one?" "Because," he replied, "when I was young myself, I did not love old women, and cannot hope, that now I am old, a young woman can love me"(*Gul*. vi. 8).

Instead of the comforts of a family circle Sadi was doomed to pass the sixty or seventy last years of his extreme long life in the cell of a hermit, and latterly seems to have imbibed a reprehensible portion of that ancient Grecian, as well as Oriental contempt for the fair sex, and to have entertained a prejudiced and strange notion about our posterity and the marriage duty (*Gul*. vi. 5). In *Gulistan* viii. 55 he says —"*Consilium foeminis invalidum*: it be bad to hold counsel with women", or, as he adds on another occasion, "take your wife's opinion, and act opposite to it !" And again (*Bust*. vi. 24), "Choose a fresh wife every spring or new year's day, for the almanack of last year is good for nothing!" According to the Mussulman creed, prayers five times a day bring the good believer half-way towards the Deity, and in this, as absolutely necessary to corporal purification, ablution is each time included, but with women certain physical impurities (*Bust*. ix.13), prevent this ceremonial for some days monthly; yet Sadi adds those do not, according to our European vulgar notion, exclude women from Paradise. Nor, though he recommends selfishness (*Bust*. ii. 7)—"Because the property of my father descended to me, it needs not be left to descend to my children. Eat and drink, spend and enjoy it thyself, for why shouldst thou trouble thyself about those who are to succeed thee;" yet he carries not this misanthrophy so far as our prince of existing fashionable poets has done.

But amidst the crowd, the hum, and shock of men,
To hear, to see, to feel, and to possess,
And roam along the world's tir'd denizen,
With none who bless us, none whom we can bless;
None with kindred consciousness endued:
This is to be alone, and my lov'd solitude!

That he was not a domestic man and had no surviving family, was no fault of Sadi. Like Socrates he put wedlock to the double ordeal of a trial; and if he enjoyed not the social retirement of a Solon, he felt not the misanthropic celibacy of a Thales. After those experiments he prided him in his tempered kinaat or contentment, and supported himself with unaffected indifference, on the casual charity of his admirers during the two last third parts of his life, either as a wandering mendicant or solitary recluse. "Never," does he honestly exclaim (*Gul.* iii. 19), "did I complain of my forlorn condition but on one occasion when my feet were bare and I had not wherewithal to shoe them. Soon after meeting a man without feet, I was thankful for the bounty of Providence to myself, and with perfect resignation submitted to my want of shoes."

Many such anecdotes, incidents, and adventures, that occurred to him during his travels, we meet in his works, and, whether creditable or not, told with the same ingenuousness. Crimes, vices, and misfortunes chiefly occupy the narratives of such adventurers among ourselves, but even in romance the hero's life generally concludes in his first wedlock. Our rigid law would construe Sadi's adventure with the Brahmin at Sumnaat (*Bust.* viii. 15), and Moses' slaughter of the Egyptian into murder; otherwise, however unfortunate, his personal adventures seldom have the stain of crime, or even vice. Nay, after he had ceased to be a married man and enterprising traveller, his life continues to interest and himself to be useful, for, as an Ascetic, he was visited by the first characters of his time, and consulted by his contemporary princes and kings.

Dowlat Shah says "that the first thirty years of Sadi's long life was devoted to study and laying up a stock of knowledge; the next thirty, or perhaps forty, in treasuring up experience and disseminating that knowledge during his wide-extending travels; and that some portion should intervene between the business of life and hour of death, and that with him chanced to be the largest share of it, he spent the remainder of his life, or seventy years, in the retirement of a recluse, when he was exemplary in his temperance and edifying in his piety." Even when a boy he confesses himself to have been overmuch religious (*Gul.* ii. 7), and ingenuously mentions this reproof of his father – "You had better," said that sensible parent, "have been yourself asleep than to be thus calumniating your neighbours." In *Gul.* v. 18 he says "that on the death of a young friend, and himself still a young man, he had vowed to pass a life of retirement, and to fold up the carpet of enjoyment." And in the preface of the *Gulistan* he is enticed by another friend to quit such a state of abstraction and retirement. He would seem to have been sincere and affectionate in his friendships; and many such disappointments, and an habitual love of seclusion, had often disgusted him with social life, and early inured him to the habits of a hermit (*Gul.* ii. 30). However, real want, I fear, had often brought him back into the busy world, for he positively tells us,

Paupertas impulit audax
Ut verses facerem,

That he wrote for his bread. *Bustan* vi. 5 — "The belly puts manacles upon the wrists, and fetters upon the ankles; the bounden slave of the belly is constrained in his devotions; had Sadi's belly in any shape resembled his back — that is, been tolerant of its load, nobody would at this day have been criticizing his writings." And, in *Bustan* vii. 6, he alludes to his having commenced to write at a late period, and that having once begun, he had no alternative but that of proceeding.

Jami relates "that Sadi had travelled much and far, and visited many strange countries. He had often made the pilgrimage of Mecca on foot, and once penetrated so far as the *pagoda,* or *botkadah,* image-temple, at Sumnaat, on the Malabar coast, were he overthrew, and broke in pieces, the great idol. He had much religious and moral intercourse with Shaikh Shohab-ud-din and other reverend gentlemen. For a length of time he led the life of a sacayi, or water-drawer, in the Holy Land, and was thus administering to the thirsty traveller, till found worthy of an introduction to the prophet Khizr, Elias or the Syrian and Greek Hermes, who moistened his mouth with the water of immortality. A descendant of Ali disputed the truth of this with Sadi, and got reproved in a dream by the prophet for his incredulity. Another gentleman had also doubted it, and next night had a dream, or rather vision; for it seemed to him as if the gates of heaven were thrown open, and a host of angels descending with salvers of glory in their hands. On asking one of them for whom those were intended, he answered for Shaikh Sadi of Shiraz, who has written a stanza of poetry that has met the approbation of God Almighty," as follows — To the eye of the intelligent the foliage of the grove displays, in every leaf, a volume of the Creator's works:

> The meanest floweret of the vale,
> The simplest note that swells the gale,
> The common sun, the air, and skies,
> To him are opening paradise!

"On recovering from his reverie, that holy man forthwith proceeded to the door of Sadi's cell, in order to apologise for his incredulity, and to congratulate him upon this auspicious vision. He found the Shaikh sitting up, with a lighted taper before him, and chant-ing to himself; and, on listening attentively, found that he was singing the above stanza." Incredible as this is, one of the fathers of our church, St Chrysostom, tells us "that, on consecrating the element of bread and wine, he has instantaneously seen a multitude of white-robed angels surrounding the altar, and bowing their heads, as soldiers do in making their homage to the sovereign!"

In his Life of Khosraw of Delhi, Jami tells us that this poet also asked Khizr for a mouthful of this inspiring beverage; but he told him that Sadi had got the last of it. Yet Hafiz, who is on this account called Sadie sani, or a second Sadi, tells us in one of his *ghazals*—"Yesterday, at dawn, God delivered me from all worldly affliction ; and amidst the gloom of night presented me with the water of immortality !"

Sadi states himself to be at Delhi during the Patan Aglamish's time, who, after a reign of twenty-six years, died A.H. 633, or in Sadi's sixty-second year; and if Amir Khosraw, descended from the Amirs, or princes, of the noble tribe of Lachin in the province of Balkh, was, as Jami says and is generally believed, the youth Sadi, in *Gulistan* v. 17, got so much enraptured with at Cashghur, and who died at Delhi, A.H. 715, in his seventy-fourth year; allowing Khosraw to have been fourteen when they met, Sadi was still a traveller in A.H. 641, or his seventieth year!

In the course of reading his works, I have remarked that he mentions himself to have visited in person Europe, Barbary, Abyssinia, Egypt, Syria, Palestine, Armenia, Asia Minor, the three grand divisions of Arabia, and every province of Iran and many parts of Turan, or of Persia and Tartary, from Busrah and Baghdad to the Scythian Wall, and at Rudbar, Deilman on the Caspian Sea, Cashghur beyond the Jihun, or Oxus, across the Sindh, or Indus, and into many parts of Hindustan, etc.; and, from a poem in his book of Fragments, it appears that he had a practical knowledge, for he quotes a line in each, of eighteen idioms, dialects, and languages, as spoken in the many regions into which he had thus travelled.

Engelbert Koempfer, who visited Shiraz A.D. 1686, says of Sadi, "that videt Egyptiain et Italiam; and that he was much skilled in the Oriental languages; nay, that he had studied the Latin tongue, and had diligently perused the works of Seneca!" But any partiality for the blemishes of this Roman metaphysician would better apply to Jami than to Sadi.

A man of Sadi's character and fame was recollected with fondness and veneration in the many regions he thus visited; and few of them, especially those under Mussulman governments, but retain some local memorial of him; and in their collections of Persian anecdotes, and these, like our Joe Miller's jests, abound all over the East, their writers accommodate him with a niche, as he had himself complimented an Esop or Lucman, Socrates or Plato, Hippocrates or Galen, and even St. John the Baptist and our blessed Saviour! Two examples I shall here translate from his Badaya, or book of rhetorical *ghazals*; and first — "No man can in this world listen to the lamentations of Sadi that must not bear testimony to his complaints, as originating in the very extremity of pain. If Plato in his wisdom is mysterious in defining love, the veil shall ultimately be withdrawn from the face of his hidden secret."

This alludes of course to the Platonic love, which was not so much a doctrine of Plato as of his refining followers, and which the followers of Sadi construed into downright sufiasm and mystery! Again — "It is the vernal season; for the heart is every moment longing to walk in the garden, and every bird of the grove is melodious in its carols as the nightingale. Thou wilt fancy it the dawning zephyr of an early spring, or new year's day morning; but it is the breath of Isa, or Jesus; for in that fresh breath and verdure the dead earth is reviving!"

Of our blessed Saviour Sadi and all the best Persian poets often speak, and always with respect and reverence; and here, as on many other occasions, he admits of his power of working miracles, if not his divinity; and I wish I could speak as well in the converse of our Christian missionaries in the East! And in *Gulistan* ii. 10 we find Sadi praying at St. John the Baptist's tomb at Damascus, and asked by the prince of that province to intercede for him in his supplications.

In fact, Sadi was not only inspired by Khizr with the faculty of poetry, but also with that of working miracles; for Dowlat Shah tells us:

> that, when finally settled as an Ascetic, the middling and common orders of his neighbours supplied him with a daily and plenteous stock of dressed provisions, the only charity he would receive, of which he would himself sparingly partake; but the best part he hung in a basket from the balcony of his cell, that the poor wood-cutters might take it home on returning with their faggots from the wilderness. One day a thief, disguised like a wood-cutter, made free with the basket, when his arm became instantly blasted, and, with a lamentable noise, he called on the Shaikh to relieve him. He answered him in reproach: 'If you are a wood-cutter, where are the callousness and scars of your business; and if a robber, where that hardihood that would deaden your feelings to so trifling a wound?' He then prayed for, and healed him, and dismissed him with a portion of his provisions.

Nor was he on all occasions an idle traveller, for he had fought against the enemies of his faith; and, in the holy wars with the Christians and Hindus added to the name of Haji, or a pilgrim to Mecca, the epithet of Ghazi, or a holy warrior. Dastards are scurrilous; but the generous speak well even of their foes. In Bustan vii. 18, Sadi asks a brother recluse, who was railing at the Christians, "whether he had ever been engaged in the holy wars with the Franks?" Yet he can confess that, any more than Horace or Otway, he was no warrior by profession, for he and another gay youth, tricked out in all the habiliments of war, submitted to be plundered of them by two Hindu robbers in the territory of Balkh, rather than risk their lives in defending them (*Gul*. vii. 13).

Ibrahim Khan of Banares, in his *Sohofi Ibrahim*, says : "A few of the illustrious results of Sadi's extensive travels were the sight of strange cities and territories, the detail of marvellous adventures, the vicissitudes of life, conversation of enlightened sages, the acquisition of science and knowledge, and, above all, a mouthful of the prophet Khizr's water of immortality!" Or, as he says himself in his *Bustan* vi. 16 : "Was not this globe shaken to its centre before it came to rest? Was not Sadi obliged to travel before he obtained science and knowledge, the objects of his heart?" On his worldly experience I refer the reader to *Gul*. iii. 28, where a father dissuades his able-bodied son from roaming from home, and anticipates his disappointments abroad. And of his own unsettled state, whether from necessity or habit, he speaks with his usual philosophy (*Bust*. v. 2): "Fortune so ordained that I should leave Ispahan, for I had no means of subsisting any longer at that place: my destiny removed me from Irac into Syria, and in this happy land I made a pleasant sojourn: the cup of my allotted abode in Syria again overflowed, and a longing desire to see home drew me thence; and chance again ordained that, on my return, I should pass through the province of Irac."

The following story must be familiar with the Persian tyro of Bengal, being an extract of the Travels of Hatim Tayi, and the first Persian book put into his hands, and is no doubt the prototype of that wonderful German romance of Leonora, which some twenty years ago was popular in two or three able translations into English.

> On one occasion Sadi had made a long enough stay in Armenia to unite himself in the bonds of friendship with a youth of his own age. In that country people then died not the natural death they died elsewhere, but on a particular day, once a year, they met on a plain by their chief cities, where they occupied themselves in recreation and amusement; in the midst of which individuals of every age and rank would suddenly stop, make a reverence to the west, gird up their loins, and, setting out full speed towards that quarter of the desert, were no more seen nor heard of. Sadi had often remarked that this was the lot of many who were fathers, mothers, brothers, and sisters of some or other of his acquaintance; but these seemed indifferent to the event, and were reserved in explaining it. At last, on such an anniversary, he saw that friend of his affection preparing to set-off when he seized upon his girdle, and insisted upon knowing what it meant. The youth solemnly

> enjoined him to let him go, for that the Malic-al-mo-at, or Angel of Death, had already called on him twice, and on the third call his destiny would drag him on, whether he would or not. Yet Sadi kept his hold, and found himself carried along with such a velocity as soon deprived him of all power of knowing whither they went. At last they stopped at a verdant plain in the midst of the desert; when the youth stretched himself upon the earth, and the turf opened like a grave and swallowed him up !

After throwing dust over his body, Sadi sat for some days by the head of the grave; and of his manifold lamentations the following is one : "On the day when thy foot was pierced with the thorn of death, would to God that the hand of fortune had clove my head with the sword of annihilation! that my eyes might not this day have seen the world without thee; such am I seated at the head of thy dust, as the ashes are on my own head !" After this he had his way to find back over rivers of molten gold, silver, and copper, through deserts and wildernesses, and over mountains of snow, which he accomplishes after many other adventures.

During his many years of travel Sadi had to traverse a sufficiency of clime, and encountered a diversity of adventure without driving us to the shift of carrying him thus into fairyland, and making him the hero of one of his own fables; and amidst the real distress of poverty, and the dissipation of a wandering and unsettled life, he rose to eminence in wisdom and learning; for, ill supplied with the gifts of fortune, the most precious part of that life was a continued sojourn from city to city, and from kingdom to kingdom, first perhaps led by a hope of patronage and preferment, and afterwards through choice and habit. During this period, though he began them late in life, his *Kulliat*, or works, were composed; and amidst a roving activity he contrived to write more than another might, in a like condition, have managed to read.

Dowlat Shah says: "The learning and wit of Sadi have been the continued theme of the eloquent ever since his time: his works contain much variety of poetry and prose, and of the former there are nearly twenty thousand verses." Dowlat Shah lived two hundred years after Sadi, when Persian literature was upon its decline, and speaks of his fame in Asia; and in the course of 480 years more, Europe is getting a relish for him. Koempfer, speaking of Sadi and Hafiz, says "that both are held in such esteem throughout the East that he can scarce be considered as a respectable character who has not read their works, and treasured up their wisdom, so as to make them the rules of his future life". And Jami and Ibrahim Khan both tell us "that men of genius have called the Diwan, or poetical works of Sadi, the

Namakdan, or Salt-cellar of Poets; and reputable writers have declared that Sadi was inspired," in confirmation of which, Molana Hatifa, the nephew of Jami, and his superior in genius penned the following stanza: "Notwithstanding what the prophet Mohammed has said, that after me no prophet can come, yet there are among the poets three men endowed with divine inspiration — namely, Firdausi in heroics, Anwari in elegy, and Sadi in the ghazal or ode."

Mulowi Mohammed Rashid, the able and learned collator of the printed Calcutta edition, in two folio volumes, A.D. 1791-2, says in his Persian introduction: "It must not be omitted that the original collector and editor of Shaikh Sadi's *Kulliat*, or Works, was Aliben-Ahmad of Bisitun; and in the preface, which he composed at the same time, and which has ever since been the constant antecedent of the Works, he accounts for the occasion of this compilation, and gives the date of A.H. 726 and 734, or 33 and 41 years after Sadi's demise." Bisitun, the birthplace of this friend of Sadi, and the site of the statuary Farhad's operations, lies in the southern part of Irac Ajim, and on the high road from the city of Hamadan to Gilanac and Baghdad.

D'Herbelot, as in many of his other oriental statements, leads Sir W. Jones astray in making the Works of Sadi to consist of only three books—namely, the *Gulistan, Bustan,* and *Mulumaat*; and even Major Stewart, in his late catalogue of Tippoo Sultan's library, makes them to consist only of seventeen books; but Ali-ben-Ahmad more correctly enumerates twenty-two; to wit:

1st, *Rasallah,* or Tract.
2nd, *Rasallah,* or Tract.
3rd, *Rasallah,* or Tract.
4th, *Rasallah,* or Tract.
5th, *Rasallah,* or Tract.
6th, *Rasallah,* or Tract.
7th, *Gulistan,* or Flower-garden.
8th, *Bustan,* or Fruit-garden.
9th, *Arabian Casaids,* or Elegies.
10th, *Persian Casaids,* or Elegies.
11th, *Mirazi,* or Dirges.
12th, *Mulumaat,* or mixed poems of Persian and Arabic.
13th, *Turjiyat,* or poems with burthens.
14th, *Taybaat,* or plain and less mystical *ghazals.*

15th,	*Badaya*, or rhetorical and more mystical *ghazals*
16th,	*Khowatim*, or what Sadi wrote in his old age.
17th,	*Kudim*, or what he wrote in his younger days.
18th,	*Sahibiyah*, or poems of eulogy and admonition, chiefly addressed to his patron Shams-ud-din.
19th,	*Macaittaat*, or Fragments.
20th,	*Khubisaat*, or prose and poetry on impure and ludicrous subjects.
21st,	*Robiayat*, or tetrastics with regular rhymes.
22nd,	*Muffridaat*, or distiches with regular rhymes.

Of these two-and-twenty books, the six books of *Rasallahs*, the *Gulistan*, and part of the *Khubisaat*, are prose, and all the rest poetry: the *Bustan* consists of couplets, or the heroic line of Firdausi and Nizami, of ten and eleven syllables, and corresponding with that of Pope and Addison in English: the rest are chiefly *casaids*, or elegies, and *ghazals*, or odes, the first two lines forming a couplet of eleven to seventeen syllables, and the alternate lines throughout the poem rhyming to this, and in a manner peculiar to Persian and Arabic poetry. The fourteenth book, or that of *Taybaat*, forms of itself nearly a Diwan, or collection of *ghazals*; the two first lines of the first four of them terminate in an Alif and the others in succession in each letter of the alphabet. Ibrahim Khan says: "That it must not be concealed from the decorators of the poetical grove that the *ghazal* bower was first reared by Sadi !" But in this he was mistaken; for Khacani, Jabali, and many others, his seniors, write *ghazals*; and indeed the word *Chamah* in old Persian has the same signification as the Arabic word *ghazal*, as *Chaghanah* has of *Casidah*; and poems of these two forms, of the ode and elegy respectively, must have been common with the Persians from time immemorial. Now, whatever Hafiz may be, can I subscribe to Dowlat Shah's opinion "of Amir Khosraw being superior to Sadi in the *ghazal*".

In the library at the India House, London, there is a curious copy of Sadi's *Kulliat*, of a date previous to the collated copy of Ali-bin-Ahmad: it had been deposited there by my old shipmate, Sir Harford Jones, who had received it, I think, as a present during his last embassy to Persia. I had it for a few minutes in my hand in 1814; and, from the little I could thus see of it, should esteem it a valuable reference to any future publisher of Sadi's text.

I had myself a personal knowledge of the Calcutta printed edition of Sadi's works, in two small folio volumes, being collated with much skill and diligence by Mulowi Mohammed Rashid, from four valuable MS. copies, some of which I also recognized in that library; but the text one, once honoured with a place in the library of the mighty and great

Moghul Shah Jehan, is now in my possession. Of that printed copy the text of the *Gulistan* occupies nearly a third of the first volume, or a sixth of the whole, and from that I made my collated translation, and should still prefer it; but Mr. Gladwin chose, as the basis of his Calcutta edition, the text of Gentius; and a reprint of that having been made in London, 1809, under the superintendance of Sir Gore Ouseley, and patronized by the professors of the East India Company's colleges, and my chief view in this translation being to facilitate the studies of their Persian pupils, I was under the necessity of modelling it to their taste. Any particulars I shall specify in a memorandum at the conclusion of this Essay.

Sadi had a personal acquaintance with some of the principal poets and literary characters of his time: some, however, and particularly he and Jilal-ud-din Rumi, commonly known as the Mulowi Manowi, or mystical doctor, and equally patronized by Shumsud-din, the prime minister of Abaca-an, make no mention of each other. Hakim Nizari and Sadi meeting accidentally in the market-place at Shiraz, and having some conversation, each soon recognized a mutual poet in his wit; and Sadi having of course invited him to his dwelling, and happening to be flush of cash, most sumptuously entertained him. Some time after they met in Khorasan, where Nizari in turn received Sadi as his guest; and, as a satire on his prodigality, the first day treated him with a pot of boiled milk and bread, the second day with a dish of fish, and the third with a joint of roast meat, observing to him at the same time: "I can afford to entertain you thus for years; but the expensive style in which you entertained me could not have lasted many days." Yet Nizari was in fact an epicure, drunkard, and debauchee; whereas Sadi was habitually temperate, sober, and chaste. When Sadi met him at Shiraz, he asked whether he recollected any of Nizari's verses; and he answers him by quoting the Motla, or first stanza, of one or his own *ghazals*: "It was rumoured abroad that I was penitent, and had forsaken wine; but this is a gross calumny, for what have I to do with repentance?"

Swift, Sterne, and other wits of our last and the preceding age, could relish indecency and nastiness; and it is creditable perhaps to the present generation that it has no taste for such grossnesses. This was not, however, the case in the age and country in which Sadi flourished, any more than it was in the early and best parts of our own literary history. The works, not only of Sadi, but of many other Persian poets and moralists, afford too many examples of coarseness and indelicacy, both of thought and expression; and, what is singular, Firdausi, Nizami, Khacani, and all their best heroic poets have scarcely any of them. Nor is it in his *Khubisaat*, or book of professed impurities, that Sadi thus violates decency; for even the morality of the *Gulistan* and *Bustan* is occasionally tarnished with such indecorus allusions: but, in this way, of all the Persians Sozni, a vigorous writer otherwise, is the greatest culprit!

On my way to Europe, having occasion to pass the months of December and January 1796-7 in Calcutta, I put my translation of the Gulistan into the hands of my friend Mr. Gladwin, wishing to have his opinion of it; when he told me he had also projected a translation of it, and meant to obviate another indelicate allusion, particularly in the fifth chapter, by changing the male for the female character. That I see he has done; and he has otherwise endeavoured, by castrating the English of it, to purify Gentius's text. But he has overlooked the occasional instances of grossness and indelicacy of sentiment and expression to which I allude above; and which I have obviated by the simpler process of leaving out the translation of a few words of the Persian text, the first example of this occurring in Gulistan i. 40. However, in all such instances, it has been my endeavour to preserve, as much as common decency will permit of it, the English of Sadi's text, that the college student may not be disappointed; particularly as the author would seem here alone to indulge in obscurity. For such passages — "Nudi enim sunt, recti, et venusti, omne ornatu orationis tanquam veste detracto"— the best apology I would offer is the simplicity of heart and nakedness of diction of Oriental writers, examples of which occasionally occur in our Old Testament; and them the profound scholars of James's reign, conscious of purity themselves, translated into downright and intelligible English; and, if I am in any instance, with the view of being intelligible in like manner, coarse, let the reader skip over it, as some of our queasy clergy do in reading the morning and evening lessons. Yet — *horresco referens* — I must not overlook another propensity to which Sadi is accused of alluding with a reprehensible levity. An example of this nature occurs in *Gulistan* v. 20, where the Cazi of Hamadan, a character in the East equally venerable and sanctified as a Judge or Bishop with us, is in the first instance sentenced to condign death and annihilation, but afterwards his abomination is made the subject of wit and repartee. But whatever levity he may sport, it in no instance appears that he criminally countenanced, and still less, as some, who have slightly inspected his works, suspect, practised this vice; for on other occasions he speaks of it, and its abettors, with all due scorn and abhorrence—a notable example of which occurs *Gulistan* iii. 14.

In the Kholasah-u'l-Ashaar, from which I also copied the above story of Nizari, it is related "that Kh'ajah Humam-ud-din of Tabreiz, or Tauris, had a son exquisitely handsome; and that Sadi, who was a great admirer of human beauty, travelled to Tabriez that he might see him. He was one day in the public bathing-room at Tabriez, when the Kh'ajah entered, accompanied by this son; and as he always concealed him from public view, he was offended at meeting Sadi, and asked him, "Whence come you?" Sadi answered, "From Shiraz!" "It is singular," said Humam, "that in my city the Shirazians should be more than the dogs and cats!" "In my city," replied Sadi, "it is the reverse; for there the Tabriezians are less !" Like many of his townsmen, Sadi was bald. Humam turning the ewer he was using, as is customary in Oriental ablution, upside down, asked Sadi, "How comes it that the head of a Shirazian should resemble this utensil ?" Sadi promptly answered him by presenting his own ewer with the empty mouth upwards, and saying, "Why is the head of a Tabriezian so very like this?" The Kh'ajah, who was himself a poet, and gentleman of considerable eminence and fortune, was vexed at these two smart replies; and, making his son sit down behind him, asked Sadi, "Have you ever heard of any of Kh'ajah Humam's poetry at Shiraz?" Sadi answered, "Yes;" and repeated this fragment — "Humam is a veil between me and my beloved; but the hour is fast approaching when that too shall be removed." The Kh'ajah was now made aware that this could only be Sadi; and, having made him the usual compliments of marked respect, took him home to his mansion, where he continued for a length of time absorbed in contemplating the charms of the son. D'Herbelot, in his *Bibliothêque Orientale*, 414, quotes Lamai's Duftar-u'l-Lataif, or record of witticisms in the Turkish language, as his authority for one of the above repartees, and says: "The veil here alluded to is the human body, which prevents our seeing God; and that by this verse he-namely, Humam-intimated his approaching death." And in Ibrahim Khan's relation of it there is a play upon the word Kun, no uncommon thing among modern Persian scribblers, but which decency again forbids me to translate.

We are told in the Sayr-u'l-mota-kharin, or modern history, of Gholam Hosain:

> That among other men of rank and education who fled from Persia in Sadi's days, in order to escape the rapacity and cruelty of the illiterate Jinghiz Khan and his Tartar successors, were Amir Khosraw and Amir Hasan, both poets of genius and learning; when they found an elegant and literary retirement with that accomplished prince Sultan Mohammed, the son of Giyath-ud-din Boltan the Guri King of Delhi, who in his father's life-time held a sort of sovereign authority over Multan, and other Hindustani provinces bordering on Persia; in defence of which he afterwards, A.H. 683, A.D. 1284, fell fighting gloriously in battle. One day those noble exiles were holding forth, in the presence of their munificent patron, on the wit and erudition of Shaikh Sadi of Shiraz, which both were so liberal in praising, as to induce the Shahzadah, or heir apparent, to depute a special messenger with many valuable gifts to the Shaikh, and an invitation to come and reside at Multan, where he engaged to build him a monastery. and endow it with villages and lands; but Sadi, because of his extreme age and feeble frame, being then in his ninety-second year, declined this

> friendly offer. However, in return for the prince's handsome attention, he sent him a volume of pleasant and elegant verses, and the *Bustan* and *Gulistan* copied with his own hand; and like a man of real learning himself he had the generosity of availing himself of this opportunity, 'to recommend Amir Khosraw to the prince, and bestow a candid approbation on his works,' which, by-the-bye, are very voluminous, for his poetry alone consists of between 400,000 and 500,000 verses!

I shall quote one more instance of the respect in which Sadi was held from the sixth *Rasallah* of his own works, where it is called his interview with Sultan Abaca-an, then king of Persia.

Sadi tells us, saying:

> When on my return from a pilgrimage to the holy Mecca, I arrived at that seat of sovereignty Tabriez, and had enjoyed an intercourse with some learned and pious men, whose society did me much honour, I got desirous of seeing those two illustrious noblemen, Kh'ajahs Ula-ud-din and Shums-ud-din, as many claims of friendship had of old subsisted between us; and having set out one day with the view of calling on them, I chanced to meet them on my way, riding on horseback, in company with Abaca-an, the sovereign of the universe. Seeing them so engaged, I did not judge it proper to intrude upon them with a friendly visit; and was in the act of taking myself aside, when they both dismounted, and, following me on foot, bowed themselves to the earth; and, on coming close up to me, kissed my hands and feet; and, congratulating this wretched creature on his safe arrival, said this was not just that we had not been apprised of the auspicious approach of our august and venerable father — After attending to this ceremony, Sultan Abaca-an remarked — How many years has Shums-ud-din been in my service, and has known me as the sovereign of the universe, yet he never made me such homage and respect as he has shown this man? And on the two brothers rejoining him, and remounting their horses, he turned round to Shums-ud-din and said, 'Who is that person whom you accosted so humbly, and received so civilly? Shums-ud-din answered, 'O Sire! this was our father !' Then the Sultan said, 'Oftentimes have I asked after your father, and you were answering

> me, he is dead; and now you said, this was our father !' He replied, 'He is our father and our Shaikh; possibly the renowned name of Shaikh Sadi of Shiraz may have reached his royal highness's ear, for his sayings are celebrated all over the world.' Abaca-an commanded them, saying, 'You must introduce me to him.' They replied, 'We have heard and shall obey.'

Accordingly, after associating with the Shaikh for some days, they asked him to attend the king; but he was declining their invitation and saying, "Relieve me from this ceremony, and make my excuses." They said, "You will assuredly go for our sakes, and shall be your own master in every matter else." The Shaikh adds, "For their satisfaction I agreed to accompany them; and having attended at court, and had an audience of the king, when about to take my leave, his majesty was pleased to say, 'Give me a maxim of advice.' I replied, 'You can take along with you, from this world into the next, nothing but reward or punishment; now, or in this world, be thou charitable and righteous ! "Abaca-an said, "Put the purport of this sentiment into verse;" and the Shaikh uttered this extemporary fragment on Equity and Justice: "That king who is the pastor of the people, let his revenue be sacred, for it is the hire of the shepherd but if not the people's guardian, let it be his deadly poison, for whatever he exacts is an imposition on the faithful." Abaca-an wept, and repeatedly asked, "Am I that pastor or not?" And the Shaikh each time answered, "If you are, the first couplet is in favour of your case, otherwise the second literally applies to it." The Shaikh adds that, "On taking my final leave, I repeated these few verses: 'A king is the shadow of God, and a shadow should be the image of its principal; the disposition of the subject is not capable of good unless it be restrained by the sword of the sovereign. Any peaceable demeanour that is found in this world originates in the justice of its princes. That sovereign's government never can be just whose entire judgment is founded in wickedness." Which met Abaca-an's fullest concurrence. Ali-bin-Ahmad adds, "That in his days pious and learned men would not venture to admonish even a common shopkeeper after this manner, and that in matters of right the times had degenerated to what they then were."

Thus have moralists in all ages complained of the degeneracy of their own days; and occasionally ventured on such advice. — Agatho, the poet and friend of Euripides, admonished Archelaus, king of Macedon, saying: "A prince should keep in mind three maxims: 1st, that he rules over men; 2nd, that he ought to rule according to law; and, 3rd, that he cannot rule for ever !" Also, it is proper to warn the reader that there must have been two Shumsuddins – one of the minister of a king of the Atabak Dynasty, who reigned at Shiraz, and patronized Sadi's father, and another the Diwan, or prime minister of Abaca-an A.H. 663,

680, by whom he was employed in offices of great trust, but was put to death, A.H. 683, by the son and successor, Sultan Arghun Khan, on the strange charge of having poisoned his father Abaca-an, and such a circumstance must have tended to embitter the latter days of Sadi.

Yet why should he regret the death of his illustrious friend and patron, who if a good man only went before him to be happy, where he, as a good man himself, and long dead to life's enjoyments, might hope, nay, wish, soon to join him. Early or late we must all go; and the heartiest and most sanguine of us is as much dead to that part of his life that is gone as that friend then was, and must soon be to what remains of it. Sadi's life was unusually long, but the latter part of it was, I fear, too unhappy for him, like the old Persian (*Gul.* vi. I) he was called upon to visit at Damascus, to regret his at last parting with it.

And, at its best, the longest life is but a drop of rain falling from a cloud into the ocean of eternity, where it is swallowed up and lost in this immensity, unless it find the body of a Sadi to nurture it into that pearl the *Gulistan* in its original classical Persian. This I have attempted to translate into English; but it is a translation, and, in order to make it useful, necessarily a literal one ; therefore the reader must not be disappointed if he find the bright water of Sadi's pearl again evaporated into the clouds, and little else left but the shell that once contained it. Yet will my object be obtained if this translation shall enable the young student to understand Sadi's Persian text, and, by relishing such a classic, recover that pearl which I was forced to drop.

However much his biographers vary in the specific number, they all agree in making him above a hundred; and Dowlat Shah and Ibrahim Khan say that Sadi lived a hundred and two years. But Jami, who was Dowlat Shah's contemporary, and as a brother poet more interested in the exact truth, states him as having been born at Shiraz, A.H. 571, or A.D. 1194, and as having died at the same place, A.H. 690; by which it would appear that he reached the very advanced age of one hundred and twenty lunar, or one hundred and sixteen solar years! This date of his death Dowlat Shah also confirms; for he says "that Sadi departed this life at Shiraz, in the reign of Atabak Mohammed Shah, the son of Muzuffar Silaghur Shah-bin-Saad-bin-Zungi, and that a dear friend records the date of that noble personage's demise as follows : "It was on the evening of Friday, or the Mohammedan Sabbath, in the month Showal, of the Arabian year 690, that the eagle of the immaterial soul of Shaikh Sadi shook from his plumage the dust of his body." This sublime sentiment was no doubt borrowed from the following two lofty couplets of Sadi's own (*Bust.* vi. I): "Now that the falcon of his soul would tower into the zenith of the sky, why hast thou burthened his pinion with a load of covetousness? Hadst thou released his skirt from the talons of carnal desires he would have soared on high into the angel Gabriel's abode." In fact, a dozen equally appropriate and beautiful epitaphs might be selected from his works. As in some parts of Scotland, it is customary with the people in the East to plant rose-bushes and other flowering shrubs round the plain graves of their defunct friends, in allusion to which Sadi says (*Gul*. vii. 16): " 'Alas! I said, 'how grateful didst thou prove to my heart so long as the verdure of thy existence flourished in the garden.' 'Have patience,' he replied, 'O my friend! till the return of the spring, and thou mayst again see verdure and flowers shooting from my bosom," Or, as my own master in rhetoric, Doctor Beattie, beautifully expresses it:

Nor yet for the ravage of winter I mourn,
Kind nature the embryo blossoms will save;
The roses shall bloom round my mouldering urn,
And spring again dawn on the night of my grave.

But these last couplets of *Bustan*, iv. 16, are still more appropriate:

> Take heed ye that tread on my ashes; by the dust of the generous I crave your remembrance, that though Sadi be mouldered into dust, what has he to apprehend who during his lifetime had also been humble as the dust? In helplessness he laid his body prostrate on the earth, and then he encompassed the globe like the wind (by travelling over it). It may soon happen that the earth shall consume him, and the wind may again whirl him like dust round the universe! Behold, while the rose-bower of mysticism blossomed in it no nightingale warbled so melodiously; now it were strange, when that nightingale is dead, if roses did not spring from its bones.

Dowlat Shah says that Sadi's tomb is situated in a charming spot, in the midst of fountains and buildings, and is held in much estimation as a place of pilgrimage; and Ibrahim Khan speaks of it under the name of Sadiyah, but he means, I fancy, that gate of Shiraz which formerly led to it. Koempfer mentions those buildings to be the numerous cemeteries of other great and learned men, and among them that of Hafiz; but the whole was in his time, A.D. 1686, rather neglected and dilapidated. My friend, Colonel W. Franklin, found it, in A.D. 1787, "just in the state it was in when Sadi was buried", and as Koempfer had found it, with the sides engraved with many sentences in the old Noskhi character, which neither of those gentlemen thought of copying. The Colonel visited it in Karim Khan's time, a great adorner of Shiraz and that neighbourhood, who built a new monument for Hafiz, but left Sadi's as it was; however, he needs no such frail support, for in his literary works he erected a monument which, like that of Horace, must outlast the pyramid!

With respect to the externals of Sadi's person, from some pictures of him in a richly-emblazed copy of his works, now in the library at the India House, and one of the four I mentioned above, his head is represented as bald, and illuminated with rays of glory. From different passages of his *Bustan* and *Gulistan* we may judge that his stature was low, and habit of body spare and slim; and from a carelessness of dress, too common with literary men, a person naturally compact, carried, from its smallness, a mean and perhaps shabby look (*Bust*. iv. 6). In order to cover such defects with the least trouble to himself, he wore over his inner garments the Kharcah-moshayakh, or long blue gown of the Darweshes (*Gul*. iv. 19); and, in the picture adjoining to his tomb, Colonel F. found him represented in this dress, with a pastoral staff in his hand, another emblem of a pilgrim and hermit.

Like the Menippian and Varronean satire, of which Petronius, Seneca, and Boetius were the chief Latin composers, and Colonel Forrester's Polite Philosopher is an example in English, the *Gulistan* is written partly in prose and partly in poetry. Better than twenty years ago I sent to our Asiatic Society at Calcutta an Essay on the Coincidences of the Oriental and European Apologue, the former chiefly extracts of Sadi's works, and particularly of the *Gulistan*. To the Apologues of this I give a more epigrammatic form by leaving out the poetry, which is in fact only a repetition in most instances of the sentiment as expressed before in prose. Part of that Essay appears in the *Asiatic Annual Register*, xii. 403, 416; part, or the whole majlis and fifth sermon in the *Bombay Literary Transactions*, i. 146, 158; and part in the *Asiatic Journals* of April and June 1817, April and June I8I8, and December 1821.

The MS. copies of the *Gulistan*, used throughout the East India Company's Empire of Hindustan as a common school book, three of which I have in my possession, are perhaps a sixth part larger than what is there called the Balaat, or the Calcutta printed text of 1791; partly in consequence of absurd insertions of many corresponding passages of Sadi's other works, and partly from foreign interpolations.

The Rosarium Politicum of Georgius Gentius, published at Amsterdam A.D. 1651, with a Latin translation, I had in my possession for some years, and found its Persian text agree more with the Calcutta printed copy than with any of the common Bengal manuscripts. A few small additions and corrections, which indeed I have made in the margin of my own copy of it, would improve it much; and if there should be a demand soon for a reprint of this textbook, as used in the Company's colleges, I am also ready to superintend it, and prevent such frequent errors as the two last lines of the first pages or a fitrat of prose being mistaken and written as poetry; and the second line of the next bayit, or couplet, having three feet of its text omitted! *The Persianischer Rosenthal of Olearius* (Schleswig, 1654) I never saw.

Commentaries and keys of the *Gulistan*, after the plan of our *Clavis Homerica*, have been composed both in Persian and Arabic. One of them, called the *Sharahi-Gulistan*, I also had once in my possession, and Mr. Gladwin showed me one in Arabic; likewise he gave me a MS. copy of the notes, as numbered for Gentius's Rosarium, but omitted in my copy; all of them, however, seemed to me equally bald and uninteresting.

Few authors are more original in their compositions, more just in their conception of a subject, or more fortunate in their choice of an expression than Sadi. Yet he is a mannerist *sui generis*; not as implying a servile imitation of any preceding admired model in Persian, but as constantly recurring to a manner of deliverance peculiarly his own. Perhaps Firdausi is the only Persian author exempt from this charge of either copying others in his characters, or of being the mannerist of himself. He has as many distinct warriors, for example, as Homer and Virgil have put together; yet his Zal-zar and Rostam, his Sohrab and Ispindiyar, have their appropriate characteristics and epithets, and are distinguished from the warriors of all other poets, and from each other; and so it is with his females, for no critic would think of confounding Rudabah, Tahiminah, the Gord-afrid, or Shirin with each other; and in expressing himself, his favourite mode is either pathos or sublimity, with an unaffected hardness, the special gift of real inspiration, whereas Nizami, whose favourite mode is energy and strength, combines withal a brevity and obscurity which act as a constant drawback otherwise on the vigour of his language and philosophic justness of his reflections; and Mulowi Manowi, whose favourite mode again is enthusiasm and rapture, has such a perpetual medley of carnal and divine love, and tendency to a re-union with the Deity, as resolves everything into sufism and mystery. On the other hand, Sadi's favourite mode is a simplicity and tenderness of heart, a delicacy of feeling and judgment, and that exquisitely natural vein in which he relates his many apologues and parables with a sort of sententious and epigrammic turn. Where, however, like the Greek epigram, the point is so very fine that, in order that his European reader may perceive and feel it, his translator must give it some substance, otherwise this manner, constituting the very essence of his original, shall entirely escape him. This I have in my translation endeavoured to catch; and if I have transgressed in one part of it more than in another, it is in making my author appear more sententious than he really is.

Engaged in such a task, a translator finds considerable difficulty in transferring this real manner of his author with spirit and fidelity, even from one language of Europe into another, and still more from an Oriental language, having the additional obstacles of a change of manners, customs, laws, and religion to encounter by the way. There are two ways of turning the sentiments of an author from one language into another—namely, translation and imitation, and Pope with ourselves tried both; and, in his imitations of Horace's Satires and Epistles, is thought to have succeeded; but, as Bentley told himself, his translation of Homer, though a very pretty poem, can, to a person that does not understand the original Greek, give no idea of Homer. Cowper says it is impossible to give in rhyme a just translation of any ancient poetry of Greece or Rome; and still more of Arabic and Persian. Cowper tried his hand at Homer in blank verse, and was still more unfortunate than Pope. A translation, to succeed, must not violate simplicity on the one hand, nor sink into tameness on the other; and, for this purpose, a prose translation, even of poetry, is preferable either to rhyme or blank verse.

But a perfect idea of any author can be formed only by understanding him in his original, and for this purpose all such translations and imitations as those of Pope, and we have an abundance of them done out of all foreign languages into English, are of little or no use; and as my chief object is to assist the young student at the East India Company's colleges in his translations, this translation of the *Gulistan* is rendered as literal as the idioms of the English and Persian language will admit; and, fortunately I have found a greater similarity in their idioms than our European critics are aware of. I shall not say how many translations I have made of the *Gulistan*, but I have now five lying by me, each done at a distant interval from another, and I am surprised how little they differ. True translation is in composition what expression is in painting; and by thus seizing the various attitudes, gestures, and looks of my Persian text, I think I have embodied them into an uniform and general design, and after frequent inspections am not displeased with my English result.

During the sixteenth and seventeenth Christian centuries, with the view of translating the Scriptures, our English doctors turned their minds to Oriental learning, many of them became proficients in the sister dialects of Hebrew, Syriac, and Arabic; but, finding the Persian so different from those three in idiom, though otherwise much the simpler and easier language, they had little or no knowledge of it. Accordingly, Bishop Walton's first edition of the polyglot scriptures, which he dedicated to Cromwell, has no Persian text, the four Ingil, or Evangelists, in this dialect having been added afterwards to the edition dedicated to Charles the Second. When the great Moghul Acbar, A.D. 1580-90, applied to the Pope for a copy of our Scriptures, he asked only for the Tawrit, or Pentateuch, having already, he said, copies of the Psalms and Evangelists in Persian, and this last was what Bishop W. or some of his coadjutors had got through the Germans. But it is not so well known in Europe that copies of the Zabur, or Psalms, were also common at that time in the East, in the Pahowi dialect, in which Nizami specifically states David to have written them!

Nor is it generally known among us that no two languages differ more in idiom and words than the Persian and Arabic; yet when Persia was subdued by the immediate successors of Mohammed, they made a special point of forcing their language, as well as religion, upon their new subjects; but after three centuries of this unnatural tyranny, on the decline of the Khalifat, the Persians, under native princes, recovered not the Pahowi, which had been the court dialect during the Sasan dynasty, but the Parsi, which had been the dialect of the Kayan dynasty, and I fancy all along the current dialect of Persia; and, in the Gulistan, Baharistan, Nagaristan, and other popular prose Persian classics, the Parsi and Arabic are, as Sir W. Jones observes, so blended "that one period often contains both languages, wholly distinct from each other in expression and idiom, but perfectly united in sense and construction, not as Roman and Saxan words are in this sentence:" "The true law is right reason, conformable to the nature of things, which calls us to the duty by commanding, deters us from sin by forbidding;" but as the Latin and English are in this: "The true *lex* is *recta ratio, conformable natura,* which by commanding vocat ad officium, by forbidding *á fraude deterreat."*

And a striking instance of this occurs in Sadi's panegyric of the prophet in the preface of his *Gulistan,* the three last lines of the second page of the Persian text being a prose medley of Persian and Arabic; the next two lines at the top of the third page a couplet of pure Arabic; the next two lines a couplet of pure Persian; and the next four lines a tetrastic of pure Arabic!

Mr. Gladwin, in his occasionally idle way, makes four distinct sentences in his English of this passage; but it is all one sentence, or, more properly, only part of one; for the same sentence also includes the parable, of which I recognise that of the importunate widow (Luke xviii 2-8) as the prototype.

Every classic scholar admires the address with which Virgil introduces his apostrophe of — *tu Marcellus eris;* and this is a happy example of the same figure of rhetoric: indeed his commencement of this graceful preface with a thanksgiving to the Deity, this praise of his prophet, his panegyric of the King, his encomium on the heir-apparent, and eulogy of the prime minister, are all felicitous instances of that *manner* which I have noted as *characteristic* of Sadi in his Persian and Arabian compositions.

The chief difficulty in translating any such Arabian quotation is its being in common a text of the Koran, or a tradition of the prophet, which though ready in the memory of a pious Mohammedan gentleman — and however much our flippant travellers and even learned doctors choose to declaim on his ignorance, a believer in the Koran can applicably quote it as the record of his law and the guide of his morals—yet, to a translator like myself; such a passage is often obscure even when complete, and still more so when only a portion of it is thus noticed, as, for example, in the *Gulistan*, i. 1, where the well-disposed Vizier says – *"such as are restraining their anger, and forgiving their fellow-creatures: and God will befriend the benevolent,"* without using the explanatory preliminary of — *"Paradise is for such as are,"* which I am, I fancy, the first who has correctly supplied by a reference to the whole in the Koran; and there we see a striking imitation of Matthew v. 3-11, where are enumerated the successive orders of good doers, for whom paradise is designed, as their ultimate and blessed place of residence!

And another constant source of trouble to a translator is the ambiguity of the Arabian moods and tenses; for not only the same tense, for example, answers for the present and future, but he is often obliged to give the preterite tense a present signification: and, if he had its immediate context, this might be managed; but with such fragments of sentences as that I have quoted, if I am obliged to adapt the Arabian quotation to the Persian context, the scholar who is capable of detecting this will I doubt not be also liberal enough in overlooking or admitting the necessity of it.

What our travellers and doctors thus assert of Mussulmans considering *Marafat*, or the divinity of the Koran, as comprehending all necessary knowledge, might have been true, as far as respected Mohammed himself; and his four immediate successors, as residents at Madainah; for we can all recollect the Khalif Omar's reply, when Amru, the conqueror of Egypt, asked him what was to be done with the library at Alexandria, he answered— "What is contained in these books you mention is either agreeable to what is written in the Koran, or book of God, or it is not; if it be, then the Koran is sufficient without them; if otherwise, it is fit they should be destroyed." But on the establishment of the Khalifat at Damascus, and still more of the Abassi dynasty at Baghdad, the Tazi, or modern Arabic, was gradually enriched with words, so as to admit of its technically expressing the terms of the arts and sciences, which a Harun Rashid had translated into it from the Persian, Coptic, and Greek; and modern Europe owes chief part of what it derived from the first two, and even more of its Greek knowledge, to translations through the Arabic, than immediately from the originals of them, or the Greek.

Whereas the more ancient Greeks, as, for instance, Hippocrates in physic, we now find copied their knowledge direct from the Persians, for all his medicines have pure Persian names; and down to the times of Galen and Dioscorides, those Greeks and their copyists, the Romans, were content with simples, which are hence called Galenicals. *Kimiya*, signifying *art, trick, imposture, chemistry, etc.*, is also a pure Persian word, which the Arabs borrowed with the art from the Persians; and the manufacture and use of chemical medicines and drugs, as applied to physic and the other arts, modern Europeans owe immediately to the

Arabs. Nay, the chemical preparations of quicksilver, now found so serviceable in all visceral obstructions, was first adopted into European practice, within my recollection, by Dr. Peasely, of Madras, in the case of Lord Pigot; and as a simple, meadow saffron root has been used lately and successfully for the gout; and I could mention a dozen other articles, each of the most active and best medicines, either for internal or external use, that have of late been introduced into our physical and surgical practice from that of the Hakims and Cub-rajes of our English empire in the East.

In the writings of Michael Servetus, who lived a century before Harvey, there is a hint respecting his curious discovery of the circulation of the blood; but the following distich of Sadi's *Bustan*, viii. 3, contains one more pertinent: "The venal system of thy body, O well-disposed man! is a meadow through which are flowing three hundred and sixty rivulets." And the two distichs, *Bustan* viii. 14, contain our most correct, and what we fancied modern, theory of respiration and digestion — "Were not the fresh air to pass by respiration into the lungs, the intestine heat would throw the body into a ferment; and did not the pot of the stomach duly concoct the food, the fair and plump form of the body would get shrunk and withered." The Persian word Khun, or blood has also the idiomatic signification of the soul and life, as existing in the blood; did the ingenious John Hunter borrow his idea of the life of the blood from this?

On the subject of aerostatics, I offer the following curious extract of my copy of the Persian dictionary, the Farhangi Jihangiri, the manuscript being itself upwards of one hundred and fifty years old: it is in explanation of the compound idiomatic word: "Tasht-wo-Khayah, the basin and egg, or the exhibition of filling the membraneous coat of an animal's testicle with Shobnim, or night-dew, and after tying up the vent, placing it on a brass vessel heated in the sun, or over the fire ; and as the air within it gets warm, the vapour will rarify and expand it; when, raising itself on one end, it will hop up and down for a while, as if dancing, and at last mount into the air, and fly out of sight!" I remember the late Doctor Black, in his Chemical Lectures at Edinburgh, 1777-8, when on the subject of factitious air, suggesting this precise experiment; but the French some years afterwards had the credit of putting it in practice on the large scale of balloons. Also, Sadi alludes to this same phenomenon in his *Bustan*, iv. 14: "Why should that befall you, which befalls the fierce-burning torch; that you should fly from yourself, as the bubble flies up from the water."

Likewise, in the Farhangi Jihangiri, in its idiomatic sense, the Fanus-khiyat, another supposed modern invention, is mentioned-namely, "A *magic lantern*, with which they show off images and figures"; and with a sort of phosphorus, or artificial fire, give them the appearance of being in a flame; and a couplet of the Persian poet Ghazali is quoted, signifying as follows — "The celestial sky is a magic lantern; and this globe is on its progress moving through it, while mankind are wandering over the globe, like the figures of a magic lantern." And would not the bulk exceed all reasonable bounds, I could quote many such sound, and what we in Europe consider as modern, hints of philosophy immediately from Sadi.

The detailed minutiae of the arts and sciences are lost in the changes and translations of languages, and in such revolutions of government as Persia has been specially subject to; yet its remaining monuments are sufficient to prove, to the latest posterity of Adam, the originality and superiority of Persian knowledge; and the value in this sense of such books as the *Gulistan*, in which glimpses remain of that knowledge.

Of the sublime and stupendous, we have in Europe no monuments of human structure that can compare with the Chih-minar, or palace of many columns, at Istikhar, the Persepolis of the Greeks; the statues of Khosraw and Shirin, and other massy works of the statuary Farhad at Bisitun, in Irac Ajem; the still more ancient images of the Sorkh-bot and Khing-bot, so called from being one of a red and the other of a grey-coloured stone, and said to be each fifty-two gaz, or yards, high, and believed by the Persians to represent their first King Gayumars and his wife at Bamiyan, near the city of Balkh, and in that part of Cabul bordering on Badakhshan; and the many sculptures and excavations in the contiguous rocks and mountains; the tower of Babel; the aqueducts of the Tigris and Euphrates; the wall of the Darband, supposed to be built by Alexander, and repaired by Nushirowan: but above all in that mode of subterraneous irrigation peculiar to Persia, and managed most ingeniously by sinking Karezes, or shafts, and connecting these with Mings, or underground canals, where springs are found at the foot of mountains, and extending for fifty or sixty miles over the contiguous champagne country.

In mechanism the ancient Persians no doubt excelled us; for even now we are at a loss to explain how such massy buildings were reared, otherwise than like our forefathers, when they first discovered many of them during the dark ages, and ascribed them to Kimiya, or magic. In the modern and more comparative architecture of the East I would refer to the mausoleum of Taj-Mahal, the favourite Sultana of the great Moghul Shah Jehan, at Agra, a building equal in extent to Saint Paul's, London, including the churchyard; and the meanest material which enters its composition is the purest white marble. Had that magnificent sovereign concluded his reign in peace, he had projected a similar one for himself on the opposite side of that noble river the Jumma; and to unite the two with a bridge of the same valuable materials: "Her bed is India; there she lies—a pearl;" but the last seven years of his life he was, by that hypocrite Aurangzib, his son, doomed to pass in honorary confinement; and having, in 1803, visited the apartments he had in that durance occupied in the palace of Agra, I had some of the plaster chipped off, and found the walls richly gilded; for, as his memoirs tell us, he had them done over with common mortar, as more suitable to his humbled condition. The centre dome had some years before been injured by a cannon-ball, and a peepal tree, one of the most destructive for such buildings, was growing out of it; but Marquis Hastings has, with much taste and at a great expense, had it since repaired, and it is now as fresh as the day, one hundred and eighty years ago, it was built. Also, the Jamai Masjid, at Delhi, is another specimen of the many elegant and modern Oriental structures which, even in the present degeneracy of the arts, rival any buildings of modern, and perhaps ancient Europe, whether we regard the symmetry of the parts or sublimity of the whole. Recent from viewing those, before I took my last passage to Europe, I had an opportunity of comparing the Governor-General's palace at Calcutta, then finished, at an enormous expense, by Marquis Wellesley, which, notwithstanding its marble hail and other pompous apartments, I found a heavy and clumsy mass of brick and mortar!

In their taste for gardening, specimens of which often occur in the beautiful descriptions of their poets, the Persians much excelled us. Milton, who travelled over the East in books, and had a judgment which qualified what he read, availed himself of those descriptions in laying out his Paradise; and Addison gave the English nation a taste for Milton, nature, and good gardening which modern Europe has since been endeavouring to copy.

The Persians have a saying, that It was as absurd for a person ignorant of geography to write history, or for a person ignorant of algebra to write upon astronomy, as for one ignorant of grammar to write poetry. In moral philosophy they excel, and particularly in what we call polite literature; no bad specimens of which are the two works of Sadi, which I have undertaken to translate—namely, the *Gulistan* and *Bustan*, and Pilpay's Fables, which are ready to follow. And as I have said, in this favourite department of literature we have frequent glimpses of their skill in the more abstruse branches of natural and experimental philosophy, of mathematics, algebra, decimal notation, and ciphering in arithmetic, of whose characters the ancient Persians were no doubt the inventors; of the phenomena of light and colours; of electricity, of which they specify many facts besides the attractive power of amber as it is detailed by our European ancients; of printing; of gunpowder and fireworks (the last is noticed by Sadi, *Gul.* vii. 14); of gems, of which they give the most rational classification we yet have, and detail some particulars in their composition of which Sir H. Davy has lately availed himself; and of their treatise on this last we have lately recovered a copy; and however vague their hints may seem at knowledge which we have not yet attained, we are from time to time obliged to give them credit for things that once appeared incredible, and which they certainly derived from sources still more ancient than themselves, and perhaps antediluvian. It is curious that what happened to the Israelites, in their conquest of the Holy Land, and the idolatrous nations they dispossessed of it, also happened to the Persians under Gayumars when they descended from the Kordistan mountains and dispossessed the Dives of Persia; and Firdausi tells us that those Dives taught the arts to their conquerors; but what is still more curious, the Brahmins of India admit themselves to be those Dives, and that they came into India from Persia.

Among the smaller articles of Persian taste I would mention three in particular: 1st. The wool, or rather hair, of a species of goat found in many parts of Persia, as well as in Tibet, from which they have from time immemorial manufactured that beautiful fabric the shawl; and to which our best staple broad cloth is so much inferior. 2nd. The murrhine vase so highly esteemed by Pliny, *Nat. Hist.*, xxxvii. 2, and which, as he correctly supposes it to be, is also the produce of Persia, and what is called with us the Portland vase is a specimen of it; and of this the late ingenious porcelain wareman, Mr. Wedgewood, energetically remarked — "that the composition of it implied a knowledge of chemistry, of which modern Europe has not yet reached the elements". Indeed our boasted chemical improvements can neither produce the materials of those sculptured and coloured vases, cups, gems, and rings, now collected by our curious travellers in Persia, nor supply any instruments of a sufficiently hard temper to cut and carve them. And, 3rd, the Sohaili, or what Europeans call Morocco leather, which forms the binding of most of the old Persian MSS., and has a fragrance and quality in it that preserves them from being destroyed by insects. This is a distinct article from the Kaimakht, another preparation of the hides of animals made in Persia into a sort of shagrin, and used for the handles of swords, dirks, etc. To prove that all those three articles are indigenous to Persia, in the Persian dictionaries they have each perhaps a dozen of names, all of them pure Persian words.

And besides them I may mention the glossy smoothness of the Yizd silks, the delicacy of the fabric of cotton into Tuz muslin and flax into Tattah cambric; their embroidery on satin, leather, and other stuffs, at Ispahan; their glass of Shiraz, or cutlery of that place and of Khorasan; their Nishampur filigree of gold and silver; their penmanship of manuscripts; the animalism at Hirat of coloured silk and cotton stuffs; the carpets of that city; the richness of their dies, and the freshness and durability of their paints, a bright and beautiful azure specimen of which I have often admired, while, in 1803, ascending into the fort of Gwalior, where it has remained on the face of the palace for centuries exposed to the open air.

Persian horsemanship and archery have been proverbial from time immemorial; and the breed of horses, camels, asses, mules, sheep, and other domestic animals, are superior to any other. Sadi, in his *Bustan* i. 1, says he met a person riding on a lion and using a snake as a whip! But, seriously, who ever thought of taming elephants, rhinoceroses, lions, tigers, and serpents, but the patient and ingenious Asiatic?

But the best use of education is that of instructing a fellow-being, which gives dignity to the creature, and enables him properly to know and respect his Creator! And what is more simple than that useful system of educating the poor which Dr. Bell has the credit of adopting from the Asiatics and applying to the European charity schools at Madras, and Mr. Lancaster of bringing into practice for the cheap and easy instruction of the illiterate of all denominations in England, and since that very generally over the continent of Europe. (See *Gulistan* vii., passim.)

These are a few of many positive facts which readily suggest themselves to any Oriental scholar, and which I, who passed twenty of the most precious years of my life in India and in familiar and daily intercourse with all descriptions of natives, and am well read in their books, set in opposition to the trifling remarks of idle sojourners and the dogmatical censures of some superficial travellers who have lately visited the East and have presumed to disgorge their ill-digested opinions upon the European world, without possessing either language or intuition to instruct it in the history and antiquities, in the laws, manners, customs, and religions, or in the literature and arts of past or present Asia.

Mankind, emerging from barbarity, fall into some regularity of government, and, getting ashamed of their ignorance, feel desirous of literary information and improvement in the arts; but before they reach any superior excellence they too often exchange the elegance of nature for the gorgeousness of art. Nor could Persia, in its many revolutions, escape such transitions; but though it suffered temporary eclipses from the barbarity and envy of such conquerors as Zohhac, Afrasiyab, Alexander, Omar, Jinghiz Khan, Timur, Nadir Shah, and Mohammed Aga, yet the basis was so broad that the column of true taste has never been totally overthrown, and has during such reigns of barbarity stood amidst a waste of apathy a monument of what had been magnificent, and served as a copy for the native dynasties of a Firedown, Kaicobad, Ardishir Babigan, Saboctagin, Alap Arselan, the Atabaks of Syria and Faristan, a Shah Abbas, Acbar, and Shah Jihan, and a Karim Khan, and Fatah-Ali Shah-shahan, to patronize and imitate.

We should recollect that the Persian is not only the sole language of the many and extensive provinces of Persia, but the medium of official and polite intercourse of the rich and populous regions of Hindustan, Turkey, and the wide domains of Tartary.

Versed as many Oriental scholars among ourselves now are in the literature and poetry of Persia, and some of them inclined like myself to communicate their knowledge, we cannot but lament that obstinacy in our English critics of taking every direct and collateral occasion of peremptorily degrading its language, as that only of conceit and false thoughts, and of rating us as admirers of tinsel instead of gold. In charity to their knowledge and their judgment, we must conclude that they speak rather of Jami and his imitators than the host of Persian poets who adorned the long period of 500 years previous to his time. If Athens had its Periclesan, and Rome its Augustan, Persia also had its classic age, not terminating in a solitary or short reign, nor confined to the narrow limits of one city or province, but extending to ten ages, and embracing places within herself a thousand miles apart.

The taste, words, and style of the language of every polished nation must suffer in the vicissitudes of time and fortune, and bad poetry will be engendered. But is Persia alone to be called to so rigid an account for the extravagance and folly of the dregs of her poets? Nay, I will admit that examples of hyperbole may be quoted from the pages of Firdausi, Nizami, Jabali, Khacani, Jilal-u"d-din Rumi, and Sadi; but if thus nice in marking every deviation from propriety of sentiment and metaphor, what would become of Shakespeare and Milton among ourselves, of Dante and Ariosto with the Italians, or perhaps of even Homer and Virgil?

A company of British merchants have established an empire of the finest provinces of Asia, nearly equal in population and extent to all Europe, where Persian is the language of law, religion, commerce, and in fact of all civilized usages; and instead of falsifying and abusing this language, our duty, as well as interest, as Englishmen, point out the justice of righting and supporting it; and let our scholars, now brought up to a classical knowledge of it at the East India Company"s colleges, endeavour to weed what they will find the current language of Hindustan of its vicious metaphors, immoderate hyperboles, silly conceits, prettinesses, bombast, and idle verbiage of the last three centuries, or since A.D. 1450, and restore it to the sublime and pathetic imagery, and the just diction of its golden age from Dakiki and Rodaki, A.D. 950, to Jami and Hatifa; and rescue it from being mangled by men learned and respectable in their knowledge of Greek and Latin, but vulgar and illiberal in their ignorance and prejudices in whatever respects the languages and literature of the East, and in particular of this scientific, diplomatic, financial, legislative, and commercial dialect of a hundred millions of our fellow-subjects! With some diffidence, I repeat that I offer the following translation of a prose Persian classic, who flourished in the era of its greatest purity; and if there is anything forbidding in the baldness of its literality, it will thus, at all events, enable perhaps the student more perfectly to understand the original; and it is only by reading that with a knowledge, that he can relish and enjoy it.

James Ross

BIBLIOGRAPHY

Akimushkin Oleg F. and Anatol A. Ivanov, "The Art of Illumination", in Basil Gray, gen. ed., *The Arts of the Book in Central Asia*, Serindia Publications, UNESCO, London, 1979, pp. 35-57.

Alam, Muzaffar, "Aspects of Agrarian Uprisings in North India in the Early Eighteenth Century", in Seema Alavi, ed., *The Eighteenth Century in India: Debates in Indian History and Society*, Oxford University Press, Delhi, 2002.

——,"The Culture and Politics of Persian in Precolonial Hindustan", in Sheldon Pollock, ed., *Literary Cultures in History: Reconstructions from South Asia*, Oxford University Press, Delhi, 2004, pp. 137-8.

Alavi, Seema, ed., *The Eighteenth Century in India: Debates in Indian History and Society*, Oxford University Press, Delhi, 2002.

Anderson, Major R.P., *The Gulistan of Shaikh Sa'di: A Complete Analysis of the Entire Persian Text*, Iran-Pakistan Institute of Persian Studies, Islamabad, 1985.

Bahura, Gopal Narain, *Literary Heritage of the Rulers of Amber and Jaipur*, Maharaja Sawai Man Singh II Museum, Jaipur, 1976.

Bayly, C.A., *Rulers, Townsmen and Bazaars: North Indian Society in the Age of British Expansion 1770-1870*, Oxford University Press, Delhi, 1992, reprint.

Brown, Percy, *Indian Painting Under the Mughals*, Hecker Art Books, New York, 1975.

Das, Asoke Kumar, *Splendour of Mughal Painting*, Vakils, Eeffer and Simons, Bombay, 1986.

Eastwick, Edward B., *The Rose Garden of Shekh Muslih'ud-din Sadi of Shiraz*, The Octagon Press Ltd., London, 1979.

Ghani, Muhammad, Abdul, *Pre-Mughal Persian in Hindustan*, The Allahabad Law Journal Press, Allahabad, 1941.

Gladwin, Francis, *The Gulistan or Rose Garden by Musle-huddeen Shaik Sady of Sheeraz*, Lok Virsa Publishing House, Islamabad, 2nd edn., 1988.

Government of Rajasthan, *Catalogue and Guide to Government Museum, Alwar*, part I, Department of Archeology and Museums, Jaipur, 1961.

Gray Basil, "The School of Shiraz", in Basil Gray, gen. ed., *The Arts of the Book in Central Asia*, Serindia Publications, UNESCO, London, 1979, pp. 121-46.

Grierson, George A., *Linguistic Survey of India*, Vol. IX, *Indo Aryan Family, Central Group, Specimens of Rajasthani and Gujarati*, Superintendent of Government Printing, Calcutta, 1908.

Gupta, Mohanlal, *Rajasthan: Zilewar Sanskritik Awam Aitihasik Adhyayan*, 2 vols., Rajasthani Granthagar, Jodhpur, 2004.

Hajek, Lubor, *Indian Miniatures of the Mughal School*, Spring Books, London, 1962.

Hasan, Hadi, *A Golden Treasury of Persian Poetry*, The Publications Division, Ministry of Information and Broadcasting, Government of India, New Delhi, 1966.

Haynes Edward S., "A Corinthian Capital on a Column of Ellora: The Transfer of the Concept of Feudalism to the Rajput States of North India", *Journal of Indian History*, 57, 1979, pp. 152-87.

——, "Imperial Impact on Rajputana: The Case of Alwar 1775-1850", *Modern Asian Studies*, 12, 1977, pp. 419-53.

——, "Patronage for the Arts and the Rise of the Alwar State", in Karine Schomer, Joan L.Erdman, Deryck O. Lodrick and Lloyd I. Rudolph, eds., *The Idea of Rajasthan: Explorations in Regional Identity*, 2 vols., Manohar and American Institute of Indian Studies, paperback edition, 2001.

Hendley, Thomas Holbein, *Ulwar and Its Art Treasures*, W. Griggs, London, 1888.

Husain Iqbal, *Early Persian Poets of India*, University of Patna, Patna, 1985.

Jain, M.S., *Concise History of Modern Rajasthan,* Wishwa Prakashan, New Delhi, 1993.

Khan, Mumtaz Ali, *Some Important Persian Prose Writings of the Thirteenth Century AD in India,* Department of Persian, Aligarh Muslim University, Aligarh, 1970.

Lodrick, Deryck O., "Rajasthan as a Region: Myth or Reality", in Karine Schomer, Joan L. Erdman, Deryck O. Lodrick and Lloyd I. Rudolph, eds., *The Idea of Rajasthan: Explorations in Regional Identity,* 2 vols., Manohar and American Institute of Indian Studies, paperback edition, Delhi, 2001.

Lotsy, J.P. and Jeremiah P. Lotsy, *Indian Book Painting,* British Library, London, 1986.

Lotsy, Jeremiah P., *The Art of Book in India,* The British Library, London, 1986.

Lowick, N.M., "Trade Patterns on the Persian Gulf in the Light of Recent Coin Evidence", *Near Eastern Numismatics, Iconography, Epigraphy and History: Studies in Honour of George C. Miles,* ed. D.K. Kouymjian, Beirut, 1974.

Lyall, Alfred C., "The Rajput States of India", *Edinburgh Review,* 1876, 144, pp. 169-203.

Misra, Neeru and Tanay Misra, *The Garden Tomb of Humayun: An Abode in Paradise,* Aryan Books International, Delhi, 2003.

Neeraj, Jeysingh, ed., *Vinay: Alwar Ank,* Raj Rishi College, Alwar, 1969.

Perlin, Frank and Burton Stein, "The Character of Old Regime Societies: State Formation and Economy Reconsidered", *Modern Asian Studies,* vol. 20, 1985.

Rajasthan State Archives, Bikaner, S. No. 746, 747; bag 107, collection 4 and 5.

Sharma, G. D., *Rajput Polity: A Study of Politics and Administration of the State of Marwar, 1638-1749,* Manohar, Delhi, 1977.

Singh, Kavita, *The Carpet of Intercourse: Courtly Etiquette in Indian Painting, Orientations,* vol. 31, no. 5, Hong Kong, 2000.

Stein, Burton, "The Segmentary State in South Indian History", *Realm and Region in Traditional*

India, ed. Richard G. Fox, Duke University Program in Comparative Studies on Southern Asia, Durham, 1977.

——, *Peasant, State and Society in Medieval South India*, Oxford University Press, Delhi, 1980.

Thorner, Daniel, "Feudalism in India", in *Feudalism in History*, ed. Rushtorn Coulborn, Archon Books, Hamden, 1965, pp. 133-50.

Verma, S.P., *Painting the Mughal Experience*, Oxford University Press, Delhi, 2005.

Vyas, R.P., *Role of Nobility in Marwar 1800-1873*, Jain Brothers, Delhi, 1969.

Welch, Stuart Cary, *Imperial Mughal Painting*, George Braziller, Pennsylvania, 1978.

Ziegler, Norman P., "Action, Power, and Service in Rajasthani Culture: A Social History of the Rajputs of Middle Period Rajasthan", Ph.D. dissertation, University of Chicago, 1973.

Zuhuruddin, Ahmad, "Shuara", in *Tarikh-i Adabiyat-i Musalmanan-i Pakistan wa Hind*, vol. 3, *Farsi Adab I (1000-1526)*, ed. Muhammad Baqar and Vahid Mirza, Panjab University, Lahore, 1971, pp. 207-37.

SOME RELATED WORKS IN ENGLISH AND OTHER LANGUAGES

Browne, Edward Granville, *A Literary History of Persia: From Firdawsi to Sa'di*, 1997.

Hämeen-Anttila, Jaakko, "Johdanto: Sa'din elämä", in *Ruusutarha* by Sa'di, tr. Jaakko Hämeen-Anttila, 1991.

Levy, Reuben, *Persian Literature, An Introduction* 1923.

Massé, H. *Essai sur le poète Saadi*, 1919.

Motaghed, Ehsan, *What Says Saadi*, 1986.

Nicholson, R.A., *Eastern Poetry and Prose*, 1922.

Phillip, Carl, *Beiträge zur darstellung des persischen lebens nach Muslih-uddîn Sa'dî*, 1901.

Yohannan , John D., *The Poet Sa'di: A Persian Humanist*, 1987.

POPULARLY KNOWN TRANSLATIONS OF *GULISTAN*

Ali-Shah, Omar, *The Rose Garden: Gulistan*, 1997.

Anderson, R.P., *The Gulistan of Shaikh Sa'di: A Complete Analysis of the Entire Persian Text*, 1985.

Arberry, A.J., *Kings and Beggars, the Five Two Chapters of Sa'di's Gulistan*, 1945.

Arnold, Sir Edwin, *The Gulistan; Being the Rose-Garden of Shaikh Sà'di*, 1899.

——, *With Sa'di in the Garden or The Book of Love*, 1888.

Burton, Sir Richard, *Tales from the Gulist?n, or Rose-Garden of the Sheikh Sa'di of Shiraz* (illustrated by John Kettelwell), 1928.

Dumoulin, James, *The Goolistan of the Celebrated Musleh-ud-Deen of Shirauz, surnamed Sheikh Sadi* (with an English tr. embellished with notes, critical and explanatory), 1807.

Eastwick, Edward B., *The Gulistan; or, Rose-garden*, 1880.

Gladwin, Francis, *The Gulistan, or Rose Garden* (with an Essay on Saadi's Life and Genius, by James Ross and a Preface by R.W. Emerson), 1865.

——, *The Gulistan, or, Rose Garden* (tr. revised and corrected by Irani A. Khodaram), 1914.

Kamran, Mohammad Kazem, *Wisdom of Sa'di*, 2001.

Rehatsek, Edward, *The Gulistan or Rose Garden, of Sa'di* (with a Preface by W.G. Archer), 1964.

Ross, James, *Sadi: Gulistan or Flower Garden*, Walter Scott, London, n.d.

INDEX